COLOR-BLIND TEACHING

Excellence for Diverse Classrooms

Daryao S. Khatri
Anne O. Hughes

SCARECROWEDUCATION

Lanham, Maryland • Toronto • Oxford
2005

Published in the United States of America
by ScarecrowEducation
An imprint of The Rowman & Littlefield Publishing Group, Inc.
4501 Forbes Boulevard, Suite 200, Lanham, Maryland 20706
www.scarecroweducation.com

PO Box 317
Oxford
OX2 9RU, UK

British Library Cataloguing in Publication Information Available

Library of Congress Cataloging-in-Publication Data

Khatri, Daryao S., 1945–
    Color-blind teaching: excellence for diverse classrooms / Daryao S. Khatri,
Anne O. Hughes.
        p.   cm.
    ISBN 1-57886-156-X (pbk. : alk. paper)
    1. Teaching.   2. Effective teaching.   3. Lesson planning.   4. Computer-
assisted instruction.   5. Teachers—Training of.   I. Hughes, Anne O.   II.
Title.
    LB1025.3.K54   2005
    371.102—dc22   2004014720

∞ ™ The paper used in this publication meets the minimum requirements of
American National Standard for Information Sciences—Permanence of
Paper for Printed Library Materials, ANSI/NISO Z39.48-1992. Manufactured
in the United States of America.

This book is dedicated to our spouses, Monika Khatri and Jack Hughes, for their tireless support and patience throughout the entire process of writing the book.

CONTENTS

LIST OF TABLES

LIST OF FIGURES

LIST OF DIALOGUES

ACKNOWLEDGMENTS

We wish to express our gratitude and appreciation to two persons who contributed significantly to the content and style of this book. First, Jack Hughes, the spouse of Anne Hughes, has been extremely helpful in providing resource advice and material. He has continued to inspire us to document and personalize our successful teaching approaches in the true spirit of "telling it like it is" in reaching and teaching diverse students to succeed in school and life. Second, we acknowledge the meticulous and thoughtful editing of the draft manuscript by Dr. Thomas Oliver, former chair of the English department at the University of the District of Columbia.

In addition, we want to recognize and sincerely thank staff members of the Scarecrow Press. First, Dr. Tom Koerner, vice president and editorial director, for identifying and supporting the publication of a book arguing that to improve the public schools, we must improve their teachers—and this means their preparation. Second, Ms. Cindy Tursman and Ms. Marjorie Johnson for effectively walking us through the publication process.

FOREWORD

In the first decade of the new millennium, one of the bigger challenges facing the nation is the ability of public education at all levels to serve an increasingly diverse clientele. This challenge must be met if the United States of America is to prepare its people to participate effectively both at home and in the international arenas. But this challenge cannot be met in a simplistic or monolithic way. As a legislator and a former teacher myself, I believe the challenge can be addressed in several ways.

First, public education must be elevated to a high priority on the national agenda. Such a priority presumes that more funding will become available for our public education systems throughout the country since virtually all of them are facing financial difficulties at both local and state levels. The federal *No Child Left Behind Act* recognizes the priority, but it is under funded; it makes scant provision for assisting under performing schools, saying only that the students can transfer and the school will be punished. But all too often, the available schools are often no better; those schools that are do not want to lower their reputations by taking in underprepared students.

Second, the *No Child Left Behind Act* has highlighted the need to place a qualified teacher in every classroom. But this challenge is not so easy as everyone is finding out. Complicating the situation still further are the changed classrooms of today: diversity is now the key characteristic. The qualified teacher for these classrooms must be able to reach and teach students manifesting a vast array of individual differences and levels of preparation. The current teacher training industry is struggling to meet the challenge of the changing nature of the classroom.

Third, alternative ways of attracting talented individuals into the teaching profession and preparing them to teach in today's diverse classrooms must be developed. Many individuals are attracted to teaching, but are daunted by the length of time and type of content required in traditional college programs. Steps should be taken to improve these programs. As part of this process, the preparation time required for motivated and discipline-qualified candidates to be ready for the classroom needs to be shortened.

This new book titled, *Color Blind Teaching: Excellence for Diverse Classrooms,* should prove to be a valuable tool for preparing qualified teachers for diverse classrooms, principally at the secondary level. And it proposes to do so in a relatively short period of time through stripping the teaching process to its essentials and then demonstrating the essentials with a hands-on content.

The authors, Drs. Daryao Khatri and Anne Hughes, have had extensive and successful teaching experience with diverse students. Indeed, all of their teaching techniques have been developed and tested through this experience. As a former teacher myself, I only wish that I could have had the advantage of this book both as someone coming into education and then later in the classroom.

Linda T. "Toddy" Puller
Member, Virginia State Senate
District 36

OVERVIEW

WHY THIS BOOK?

Color-Blind Teaching is about creating a "new" teacher at the high school and college levels for the twenty-first century—the teacher who can teach anyone, anytime, anywhere effectively, and more specifically, in the trenches of public education, like the cities. We have put "new" in quotes because there always have been some teachers who could and did teach anyone, anytime, anywhere—effectively. There just haven't been enough of them to go around, and there has been no concerted effort to train such teachers at this level. So what sets this new teacher apart from others?

This teacher

- cares deeply about teaching a particular subject matter to students—regardless of the way they look or sound.
- is fully qualified in a particular subject matter.
- finds a way to put the subject matter across to virtually every student.
- has a high energy level and never wilts until the last student has left the room.
- has well-developed social and academic skills that can inspire students.
- understands ethnic and social differences as having nothing to do with talent for learning, motivation to succeed, or hope for a better life.

This is the teacher for diverse populations: the inner-city indigenous and immigrant poverty students, the strugglers with the English language, the isolated child of the rural backwaters. This teacher does not depend upon a parent to intervene when the child is not succeeding in the class. This teacher has a calling: whatever it takes. Along the way, limits will be stretched, minds will be opened, molds will be broken, administrators will be aggravated—and children will be educated.

This "color-blind" teacher must be strikingly different from another kind of teacher who can only teach the middle-class child with middle-class parents to assist when needed in the well-supported and adequately functioning schools of affluent communities. Fortunately, for this second type of teacher, there are many such school systems. These are the systems where no one is clamoring for vouchers or charter schools. However, the adequate teacher in this system may be a prescription for student failure when students are poor, speakers of other languages, struggling immigrants, ethnically diverse, or have parents who cannot assist. The problem is compounded when these students live in a community that is overburdened or fragmented, the school system itself has become an ossified and dysfunctional hierarchy, and the teachers are overwhelmed.

Moreover, the traditional training that has produced the teacher for functioning, well-supported public school systems will not work for the diverse population this new breed of teacher must face. A different type of training is needed: one that truly prepares this person for the flat-out hard work of classroom teaching at the high school level. The training for the diverse classroom must be stripped to its essentials. These essentials must replace decorative courses characterized by verbose textbooks that bury important teaching and learning principles under arcane terminology and often oversimplified examples and taught by faculty who have rarely, if ever, worked with diverse populations. These essentials must also be used to provide new and accelerated ways to achieve a certification that truly means these new teachers function effectively in the classroom, starting on day one.

So what are the essentials for this new breed of teacher? Subject matter competency, at least at the baccalaureate level is a must, accompanied by strong verbal ability. Another is good physical health, and then there are the social and academic skills. And an old-fashioned virtue as well: dedication to the cause. Assuming you, the individual, possess all of these essentials, one more is required: the "how" of teaching, the process of communicating your subject matter—in short, the pedagogy. Stated another way, pedagogy is defined in the dictionary as "the art or the science of teaching."[1] After years of experience, we are inclined to view it more as "the art of teaching what you know." Without adequate pedagogy, your subject matter is very likely going to stay in your head rather than making the journey to the students' heads. Contrary to the avowals of many critics of the teacher training institutions and public school systems, pedagogical techniques are not "fluff stuff"; they must always be defined, demonstrated, and reinforced using a subject matter content. In the rest of this book, we will do just that.

WHO CAN BECOME THIS NEW "COLOR-BLIND" TEACHER?

We hope you can—and you will.

Actually, we think there are four audiences from which this teacher will emerge, and you are probably a member of one of them. The first audience consists of individuals who are experienced in their fields, are really interested in teaching, already have at least a baccalaureate degree in a valuable content to the schools (such as math or English), and who want to make a career change. These are candidates for fast-track alternative certification.

The second audience is composed of individuals who already are teaching and want to improve. Individuals in this group will find the pedagogical techniques described and demonstrated with hands-on experiences to be a kind of refresher or self-revitalization experience.

The third audience is classroom teachers in public school systems for whom principals and staff development professionals have determined areas of improvement that can be handled through in-service workshops and seminars. Individual chapters in this book can form the basis for workshops of varying length.

The fourth audience is that of students in a teacher training institution who are interested in enrolling in an alternative teacher certification program within a compressed time frame. Such a program would apply to either individuals in the first audience described above or the institution's own undergraduate students.

For a person doing self-training, the pace is up to that individual. For a particular school system, any of the chapters in the book can be translated into hands-on workshops and seminars in areas of particular need for teachers in that system. The school system would determine the pace. For a teacher training institution, we suggest the training can be done in the approximate three months of a summer semester or in an academic semester of approximately four months, depending upon the time frame of the program.

HOW IS THIS BOOK ORGANIZED?

The book is organized into three general sections. The first section, chapters 1 through 4, deals, respectively, with preteaching activities, classroom management tactics, and basic and advanced teaching principles. Taken together, they make up the quiver of pedagogical techniques, and they are applicable to any discipline. We, as authors, have developed, tested, and successfully applied all of them in teaching for more than thirty years, each in our particular disciplines, principally at the secondary and college levels—and always with diverse populations. Sometimes, the students in our courses resembled a miniature United Nations—but the techniques always worked. All of these techniques are defined and illustrated both by anecdotes and actual teaching dialogues with students using different disciplines. The pedagogical techniques are applicable *at any level*, with appropriate adjustments in subject matter difficulty. Subject matters vary, along with their levels of difficulty; the pedagogical techniques are the universals.

The second section, chapters 5 through 11, provides a further demonstration and reinforcement of the pedagogical techniques in action, employing universal computer applications as the hands-on experience with the techniques. The main purpose of these chapters is to demonstrate and reinforce the teaching principles and classroom management tactics through the hands-on use of a personal computer. The reader should clearly understand that the computer content is subordinate to pedagogy; these chapters do *not* comprise a manual for computer training. Again, we underscore that pedagogy can never be taught effectively without a content. A secondary purpose is to assist practicing teachers, potential teachers, and individual readers in adequately using a personal computer as a teaching device in a classroom setting. These chapters contain the computer content that has been designed and sequenced using the pedagogical techniques. The chapters include step-by-step instructions for each topic and are accompanied by a CD to be inserted into the CD drive of your computer in order for you to observe and practice all of the instructions given in the chapters. These chapters also include excerpts from actual teaching sessions (labeled as dialogues) showing the pedagogical techniques using computer content.

In the last section, the final two chapters address the increasing demands on the "color-blind" teacher today in a diverse classroom. The first of these chapters addresses the complex constants of classroom teaching for the twenty-first century: diverse populations, the art of the participant-observer, never-ending assessment, technology, and resources—there are always some—in the community and school. The last chapter talks about the twin pinnacles of the teaching process: the teachable moment (a point in time when everything comes together for the students and the teacher) and learning momentum (a steady build-up in a course toward a sometimes unexpected high point). These chapters are followed by a short finale.

So . . . read on: the best is yet to come!

NOTES

1. *Webster's Encyclopedia Unabridged Dictionary of the English Language* (New York: Gramercy Books, 1994), 1854.

GATEWAY PEDAGOGY—
PREPARING FOR TEACHING

Pedagogy, the how of teaching your subject matter, is not confined to those times when you are in the classroom with the students. No, indeed! As soon as you know what your courses are to be and generally who your students will be, the planning not only for *what* you will teach but also *how* you will teach must begin. What you teach (the actual subject matter to be taught) is often specifically stated by the department in which you will teach, but the pedagogy (how you will teach this subject matter) is usually less well specified. Here you have options and a chance to express some creativity, so you need to think seriously about how you are going to put your course content across to the crew of students who will soon be arriving on your classroom doorstep. If you are a newcomer, you need to write your general plans down and be open to changing them if they aren't working, six or eight weeks down the road. The preteaching activities are "gateway pedagogy." In other words, adopt the Scout motto, "Be prepared," as your own, but be prepared to change.

The activities described and illustrated in this chapter are designed to help you do just that. Many of these activities, if done in advance, will free you to focus on teaching your students (the course content and the supporting pedagogy). We have divided these activities into three types based on when they occur. The first group can be completed before your courses ever start. A second group of activities will need to be completed before an individual class session begins for the semester or quarter. These two groups of activities are important because they set the stage for effective teaching. The last group really amounts to judgment calls during a class session that you, in your role of teacher, must make based on the "incoming behaviors" of the students, both verbal and nonverbal, to ensure that the session continues to run smoothly.

Let us draw an analogy: these three groups of activities, in combination, are like the planning for a party. Everyone knows a well-planned, successful party involves many advance preparations, some last-minute tasks to be done before the guests arrive, and some on-the-spot innovations and adjustments to keep everything smoothly running and the guests happily participating. Actually, a party is hard work, but it can be enormously pleasurable and satisfying. Teaching is no different.

CONSTRUCT MANAGEABLE, STUDENT-ORIENTED ACADEMIC OBJECTIVES

In the first group of activities are the specific objectives for each course. These objectives identify the critical components of the course and should serve as a mechanism for evaluating whether you and your students together have achieved them. In other words, well-thought-through objectives spell out what the students are to learn and include some indication as to how the students will learn them. Accordingly, each course objective must contain two elements: "What" and "How." Together, they carry the implication of "How Well." These seemingly cryptic elements translate into the content that must be covered within the specified course time frame (the What) and the general pedagogy that will be used to communicate the content to the students (the How). If stated with sufficient specificity, the objectives will enable you to measure the extent to which you and the students have achieved the objectives (the How Well). In other words, a clear and complete objective will assist you to measure success meaningfully and help you stay focused, whereas an incomplete objective can distract you from focusing on the essentials and student success, and therefore will be hard to measure. Consider carefully the most important knowledge for the students to learn in each of your courses, and while you're at it, keep an eye on the tests they will have to face somewhere along in their student careers. Then take those important aspects of knowledge and develop an objective for each of them. You should not have more than three or four. If you do, you may be trying to include too much or you may be emphasizing too many specifics.

Some examples of clear/complete and vague/incomplete objectives for different subject matters are provided in table 1.1.

Table 1.1. Examples of Complete and Incomplete Objectives

Subject Matter Category	Incomplete Examples	Complete Examples
	Knowledge	
Mathematics	To learn exponents	To learn and apply the rules of adding and subtracting exponents with the same base when exponents appear in both the numerator and the denominator
Physics	To define physical quantities	To define and illustrate physical quantities through anchoring them to students' experiences
English	To learn the rules for commonly used types of punctuation	To learn and apply the rules for commonly used types of punctuation in nonfictional writing, such as newspapers, essays, and articles
Social Science	To learn about the disciplines comprising the social sciences	To learn about the particular focus, key theorists, and research contributions of each of the six major disciplines traditionally associated with social science, specifically, anthropology, sociology, psychology, political science, economics, and history
	Skills	
History	To memorize key dates in American history from 1865 to the present	To develop a graphical timeline to show the important themes and trends with illustrative events in American history from 1865 to the present
Sciences	To compare your answer to a problem with the key in the back of the book to see if yours is correct	To develop and practice finite steps in determining your solution to a problem instead of stating one-line answers
	Values	
English	To appreciate poems by contemporary poets	To memorize three poems by contemporary poets that have said something important to you
Psychology	To appreciate the value of theories in psychology	To appreciate the viewpoints, problems, and contributions of three major theories in psychology, such as psychoanalytic theory, gestaltist theory, and behaviorism
Mathematics	To understand the importance of algebra in the sciences today	To understand the importance of algebra in determining one's own academic program in high school, college selection, and career choices in society today
Mathematics	To encourage students to solve all the assigned problems in math and science	To encourage the use of estimation consistently in arriving at the correct answer in solving problems in math and science

Let us briefly examine these incomplete and complete examples. The incomplete examples in the knowledge category are vague and carry little indication as to how you as a teacher might proceed to teach the subject matter mentioned. The incomplete skill objectives are reduced to trivia, whereas the complete ones show the skills to be developed as being broadly applicable to various subject matters. The incomplete value objectives are fuzzy and overly general. They are likely to remain out there in the ether somewhere. The complete ones demonstrate a tangible outcome. The situation becomes even worse if incomplete objectives are handed to you as a new teacher by your department chairperson, a common practice with introductory courses at both the secondary school and college freshman levels. If you as a teacher are stuck with these similar kinds of incomplete objectives, treat them as just that and further define them yourself. Don't advertise what you have done—just do it.

In contrast, the complete examples give you clear bases for specifying the sequence of activities for your teaching sessions, the requirements for the applications, and the types and amount of practice or reinforcement likely to be required if the students are really to learn the particular topics, skills, and values identified. Complete objectives also provide the basis for knowing the extent to which students actually have learned what they were supposed to in the course. In short, complete objectives are like a road map for the trip through the course. Incomplete ones leave you on a detour.

WHAT ELSE ARE WE HERE FOR? SET SURPRISE OBJECTIVES

These objectives also fall into the first group of planning activities. Right off, you must state some "Surprise Objectives" at the beginning of the term. These objectives are focused (craftily) on eliminating problems in teaching before they can surface; put another way, you are using a preemptive strike to solve a problem before it arises. Only the objectives are stated; you do not need to advertise the problems these objectives are attempting to correct or the actions you will take in achieving them. Toward the end of the term, the teacher should obtain student feedback on how well these surprise objectives have been achieved. The teacher's actions defined in table 1.2 include both pedagogical principles and classroom management tactics.

Table 1.2.   List of "Surprise Objectives," Their Causes, and Possible Teacher Actions

Goal	Causes	Teacher Actions
1. Nobody takes a nap in this class; nobody is going to be left out.	• Students are bored or exhausted. • Teacher talks too much or for too long. • Teacher ignores the incoming behavioral signals like restlessness or sleepiness. • Too few students continually participating, typically those sitting in front. • "Swifties" clustered in front and stragglers and strugglers in the back.	• Call students by name when they least expect it, and ask for comments. • Use the differing amounts of knowledge that students possess in calling on them (differential student knowledge base). • Remember to be an observer. (You may be participating more than you are observing.) • Stop talking, comment on where you think you lost them, pause, and wait.
2. A new type of theme party just for you: the weekend study party for a Monday/Tuesday test.	• Students having difficulty in finding time to study for a test during the week.	• Schedule major tests on the first meeting day after the weekend. • Take time to assist students in forming study groups.
3. Quality study equals a quality grade.	• Students not motivated to study for tests because they are overwhelmed by assignments, homework, or unfamiliar concepts. • Poor study habits: don't read; don't review; don't take notes; don't know how to take notes; don't practice; don't do homework; don't turn off the TV: all leading to Don't Pass. • Focus by teacher is fuzzy or too sophisticated for the students.	• Make the test finite/limited. • Let students know what will be covered in the test. • Test only on what has been presented *and* taught in class. • Limit homework to specified or critical problems, such as assigning a *single* problem in sciences that is due for the next class meeting, or a single concept, method, technique in the social sciences or English. • Assign homework *only* from what has been presented and discussed in class. Never assign new or "undiscussed" material.

(continues)

Table 1.2.   (Continued)

Goal	Causes	Teacher Actions
4. Our time is prime time.	• Latecomers asking for help from other students and the teacher. • Students not listening and then asking for repeats of what has been said from either each other or the teacher. • Students reading the book and not paying attention to what is being presented. • Talking to other students and trying to get answers. • Students doing homework/studying for other subjects during your presentations or students' presentations, and then trying to catch up.	• Be a participant-observer. • Books closed during your or student presentations unless otherwise directed by you. • Provide directions one and one time only, and enforce this rule. • Tell students, "If you have a question, ask me and not another student." • Doing some other subject's work will result in a 5 percent reduction in your overall score for the course for the first offense followed by a 20 percent reduction thereafter.

PRUNING THE COURSE TO ITS ESSENTIALS

Also falling primarily into the first group of early preteaching activities is something we call course pruning. Look at any current textbook in the sciences, math, engineering, social sciences, humanities, or English. Usually, you will find these textbooks have been padded in topics, explanations, and quasi-relevant pictures that fill space but often do not enhance meaning, including wads of examples often unrelated to the experience of diverse students, and overkill in terms of problems or exercises for each chapter. Some textbooks for an introductory course in physics have more than eighty problems at the end of each chapter! An introductory social science text will usually present an extensive glossary of terms, additional readings, assorted notes, discussion questions, and other activities that are rarely used because such courses usually entail a mad gallop to cover all the ground in one semester. This padding occurs because the publishers, teachers, and administrators have been brainwashed into believing that any textbook under 500–1,000 pages in length and not printed on heavy-duty paper is not a worth its salt. An exception to this undue weightiness is Strunk and White's *The Elements of Style*, a classic book on English grammar, punctuation, style, and an absolutely delightful book to use.

In order to play it safe, many teachers will overdo the assignment of the text material as a means of covering the subject matter, so as not to look "easy." In many instances, these teachers will cover half of a chapter and assign the other half as a reading assignment to be done by students on their time (code for additional homework). Trying to cover everything is particularly true of the new teacher, and especially so if this teacher is not secure in the discipline. The bad result is the book rather than the teacher becomes the focus of the course, a complete reversal of the traditional role of a teacher. Problems and tasks assigned, usually at the end of a chapter, will be based on the entire chapter. Students thus become responsible for doing the entire set of problems or tasks, even the ones based on their own independent reading. Sooner or later, the weaker students will start to do poorly and may wind up dropping out of the course.

This problem of too much unnecessary or only tangentially related material in a book is compounded by the diversity of students who may lack much of the experiential background assumed by the text. When this lack is coupled with academic underpreparedness in the basic skills of reading, writing, math, or fluency in English, the teacher (you) faces a daunting challenge. Now, how do you tackle this challenge and still manage to teach your courses with integrity? (Case 1.1)

CASE 1.1

Here is how we do it. First off, we must recognize that we cannot do "business as usual." If we try to ignore the challenge, we will be traveling along one road and many of our students will fall by the wayside or choose an exit to escape altogether. Here is where the old adage "Start where the learner is" suddenly comes alive.

Second, we are in charge here. We must decide what of our subject matters are essential for them to learn—that is, what we qualified professionals deem necessary. In making this decision, we also have to consider what the departmental norms or tests may require as well, but we will not be enslaved by them. (In fact, we usually offer to serve on the committee that determines them, and work for a change.)

Now we come to the third consideration. Based on our knowledge of the subject matters we teach, we contend that the presentations in each chapter of a textbook can—and must—be pruned to their essential elements. Students must learn the subject matter *without ever diluting the course*, and without violating a departmental syllabus or a test. How do we do it? Here are a few general suggestions: eliminate the "interesting asides" in the text. If a picture or a graph really drives across an important concept, use it. Otherwise, forget it. The history of a subject matter is usually of interest only to you—not to struggling students. Let a subsequent course provide that. We often identify the three most important elements in a given chapter, teach them, and then tell the students that they are account-able for them. Let the rest go. Treat the text as a resource, not the God-given word. If we are teaching a gateway course, then we will need to make certain we cover whatever the students are expected to know for the next course.

This is particularly true of algebra and ninth-grade English. Having done this pruning, we find that we have much greater latitude and, of course, more time to utilize the students' experiences and knowledge as well as our own understandings of our subject matter. Also, we can spend more time reinforcing the critical elements as well.

In general, these essential elements amount to concepts, critical termi-nology and their definitions, the perspective of a given discipline, the meth-ods of study, and appropriate tasks or problems. There are all kinds of interesting ways to present these elements. "Be inventive" is our mantra! Fourth and last, we shut the doors of our classroom, do our stuff, and involve the students in the teaching-learning process—including a few side trips into reading, writing, and math if necessary—and don't worry about what our colleagues are doing. The big thing here is to keep the students traveling on the same road with us.

You can do the same.

For example, in a general social science course, the student must learn the general meaning of the term *social science*, the disciplines encom-passed, their unique perspectives, some of the major theorists and their contributions, some of the critical terms and concepts, and research find-ings for each of the disciplines involved. Such a course involves a sampling of the particular features of the disciplines involved, not a complete treat-ment. What is needed in this course is to stimulate their interest in the general nature and contributions of the social sciences. Subsequent courses in one of the specific disciplines will provide the in-depth coverage.

As another example, in an introductory physics course, the students must learn the definitions of physical quantities, the units of these quantities, and the basics of problem solving. The more sophisticated mathematical nota-tions and trivial historical facts should be left to other courses. At this level, the students do not need two hours on Newton's life history and only half-an hour (out of a total of 2.5 hours) presentation on his laws and their appli-cations.

Another way in which you can prune a course unobtrusively and ensure that you and the students are together is through the regular use of an agenda. We discuss it next.

PREPARING AN AGENDA

As we use the term *agenda*, preparing an agenda falls into the second group of activities: a task to be carried out before a particular class session. Now, everybody knows that agendas are prepared for all sorts of meetings. However, preparing an agenda for each class session is a new take on the concept of meeting. Why do we say an agenda has such an importance in the teaching process?

From the standpoint of students, the points on the agenda take the "unknown" out of the class session. That is, the students know exactly what to expect in a particular session. It also keeps the class session focused. If you are taking the "scenic route," are turning the wrong way in explaining a topic or a concept, or are drifting on to a whole different subject, the students can help you to get back on track by raising questions or by just looking lost, instead of simply enduring the digression. The agenda gives students a real stake in a class session: they are participants in a *planned* meeting.

For you, the teacher, the benefits are numerous. First, preparing the agenda forces continued planning and adjustments on your part. You must identify the topics and activities to be carried out in the class, including the assignments, instead of writing them on the chalkboard to fill the time or just plain winging it, a sure sign of underpreparedness on your part. Agenda planning typically includes an approximation of time for each of the agenda items. Including the time allocation for each item is not essential, but you should bear it in mind. For example, putting ten items on the agenda to be dealt with in a fifty-minute period typically signals you are trying to cover too much ground for the time available. The converse is true for putting only two items on an agenda for a three-hour block, unless such items have subcategories and these are included on the agenda. This practice also helps to eliminate the need for assigning too much material for the students to read independently. This is particularly necessary with underprepared and/or diverse students.

Second, whenever possible, the agenda should be prepared on a separate piece of colored paper for each major course category (large divisions within the content, tests, or major concepts). A blizzard of white is boring.

Third, the agenda allows for easy referencing for daily planning, test preparation, and pacing of the course with the particular students involved. Collectively, they can assist you in course refinement and revision.

An unexpected benefit is that the active control of the course shifts from the book to you, and you have each detail of the course at your fingertips. You become more confident as the tasks of each agenda are completed, and in turn, the presentations and class instruction run more smoothly. Also, the students respond well to the agendas, often checking off points as they are completed, or sometimes asking for additional coverage or practice. Importantly, they feel more actively involved in their learning. You always should have extra copies of the agenda available so students feel comfortable in asking for another copy, if they have misplaced theirs. Oftentimes a student will request a copy of the day's agenda for a colleague who is absent.

We have found that when we first introduce the agenda in a class, it is a novelty and an attention-getter. Many of the students we have served are older and working, and the agenda seems to put the class session into a professional setting. With the younger students, it makes them feel more important; they feel they have a stake in their learning. At the same time, the agenda sends a message that the teacher cares about them and their learning in the course. We have found the agenda becomes an integral part of the class and the group experience as well as a "course collectible." An example is provided in Chapter 4, Figure 4.1, as part of an actual teaching dialogue.

If, for some reason, the agenda is not available, usually due to duplicating problems, the students miss it, even when it is posted on the chalkboard. Also, they are apt to complain if the agenda is not on the colored paper. Like small children, students are creatures of habit, too. It has become part of their routine in a course as well as a record.

DIVIDING PROBLEMS, TASKS, AND PROJECTS INTO FINITE STEPS

The activities here fall into both the first and second groups, depending upon the magnitude of the particular activity. But, regardless of the activity, all problems, tasks, and projects, no matter how big or how small, can be divided into a specific number of finite steps. For these kinds of assignments, the steps must be sequentially organized, numbered, and labeled whenever possible. For large projects or papers, the teacher should develop a time frame for the introduction and completion of the steps, give an oral presentation of the project (including the rationale for it), and follow the presentation up with written instructions, preferably in an outline form. The first mention of these kinds of big tasks with their main steps should appear in the syllabus or the course outline. Here we give another warning: do not give the guidelines for a major project all at once. The students will be overwhelmed; they may resist and, worst of all, may not perform. First, we look at a problem in English. (See Case 1.2.)

CASE 1.2

For a term paper in English, much more is required than the topic and the minimum number of pages to be included. As the teacher, I must specify and explain the following:

1. Introduction
   1.1. Reasons for the choice of topic
   1.2. Thesis statement
   1.3. Data sources proposed
       1.3.1. Personal experience
       1.3.2. Newspapers/magazines
       1.3.3. Library materials
       1.3.4. Other
2. Body of the paper and supporting evidence
   2.1. Format
       2.1.1. Standard paragraph format—e.g., topic sentence, supporting details, and conclusion
       2.1.2. Other paragraph models, such as comparison, summary, and contrast
       2.1.3. Quotations and footnotes
   2.2. Supporting evidence
       2.2.1. Appropriateness
       2.2.2. Logical flow
3. Conclusions
   3.1. Restatement of the original thesis
   3.2. Summary of proof
4. References

For a big project like this one, the overall time frame should be at least three-fourths of a semester. Each major aspect of the paper is taught, guidelines issued for it, and students turn in drafts for my review and approval. For example, in the outline above, each part of the introduction section should be taught, illustrated, and practiced in class. Then the students prepare and submit a first draft of this section. After revisions and, based on my critique with the help of the students, the new drafts are then submitted. I have to keep after it; if this first section isn't right, the whole project is in jeopardy. When the drafts come up to an acceptable level in my judgment (I may even want to give the approved section drafts grades; the grading encourages the students to keep trying because they now know they can improve), the same procedure is repeated for the next major section. I have the students keep their drafts so they can see the tangible improvements.

Through this process, I can monitor the students' progress, teach where a common problem emerges, make the task manageable for students, and create safeguards against student failure. Doing this type of project in small groups (three is a good number) or in pairs is particularly effective with diverse and underprepared students. They can help one another, and they often show a surprising flair as well. Working in pairs or groups, these students will often feel more comfortable asking me questions than any one of them would be as an individual. This may be an application of "safety in numbers."

Now, let's examine a problem in physics. (See Case 1.3.)

CASE 1.3

The problem is taken from F. Bueche, *Principles of Physics*, 2nd ed. (New York: McGraw-Hill, 1972), 254:

"If 40 gm of ice in a 20-gm copper calorimeter can is originally at $-35°$ C, how much steam at 100° C must be condensed in this can if the ice is to be changed to water and heated to 30° C? (Given: Specific Heat of water $= 1$ cal/gm/C°; Specific Heat of copper $= .093$ cal/gm/C°; Specific Heat of ice $= .5$ cal/gm/C°)"

To solve a problem like this, at least ten steps are required. These steps are:

Step 1:   Diagram the process
Steps 2 through 7: Associate an equation to be used for each part of the diagram (there are six parts and therefore six equations).
Step 8:   Find the answer for each of the six parts.

Step 9: Put the six answers together.
Step 10: Solve for the unknown.

Because of the complex nature of this problem, walking through the problem once with the students will *not* produce mastery on their part. This type of problem must be practiced four or five times to produce a successful and independent performance by students. More importantly, the repetition increases their understanding as well as their confidence in their ability to solve complex problems.

REVIEWING, RETEACHING, OR JUST PLAIN NEW TEACHING

Now, some of the activities we will talk about here may be planned in advance of a class session, but some of them are going to fall into the third group: the judgment calls in a class session.

The educational translation of the old proverb "A stitch in time saves nine" is to review or reteach—or just plain teach, if need be—any topics or skills that students absolutely must have to be successful in the course. On the surface, students supposedly have taken the prerequisite courses, but they may not have habituated the necessary content or skills they must have for the new course. You, as the teacher, must be aware that exposure is not mastery; the teacher must review, reteach, and reinforce in order to avoid student failure and dropping out. For example:

For an introduction to a Physics II course, the students must have mastery of math skills in cross-multiplication, powers of 10, and scientific notation to ensure their success in the course. On the other hand, for an introduction to a Physics I course, the essential list is a bit longer: cross-multiplication, algebraic equations, trigonometric functions, exponents, and some basic math facts (multiplication by zero; division by zero). This list is longer because it is a prerequisite course for Physics II. Reviewing or teaching these skills should not take more than a couple of hours if the students have had exposure. If more time is needed for review, then extra time is spent on it.

Spending a couple of hours at the beginning of the course reduces student (and your) frustration levels, leads to bonding between you and the students, tips the probabilities toward student success, and increases exponentially the time available for productive course coverage. Don't give a math test as a way to find out student deficiencies; this is a surefire guarantee for creating student anxiety. When you say, "I don't have enough time to cover the course content, if I have to cover all this other stuff, too," you are copping out from dealing with student needs with regard to the course. They may start the course with you, but many of them will be gone when you cross the finish line.

Another example that involves a critical skill and is applicable across many disciplines is note taking in an outline form (See Case 1.4).

CASE 1.4

I want my students to take good notes in an outline form, so I need to make certain they know how to do it. If they don't know how to outline adequately, then I must teach them this skill. Don't assume that they learned to outline in other courses. The students may tell me they know, but the surest way to find out is to pick up their notes and compare them to my presentation. If students are just scratching down words, trying to write what I have said verbatim, and/or numbering points regardless of their significance, I—and they—have a problem with outlining. Ultimately, they will have a problem studying for tests and passing the course.

Thus, I know I need to teach them to outline, and I need to do it up front. My general pattern is to work with them on how to do a basic three-level outline as a part of their note taking. I do this through amplifying my presentation with such comments as, "I am about to begin a new topic. This is level 1 of our outline, and I will write the numeral and the topic on the chalkboard. Now you copy it." Then I make sure every student does so. "Under this topic are several subheadings or parts of the topic, which make up level 2 for this topic of our new outline. And you and I will develop some specific facts/details under each one of these subheadings." Then I proceed to do just that on the chalkboard in an interchange with the students. I lead them to see that the details or facts are all encompassed by one of the level 2 headings. Then I ask them, "How shall we handle this information, since these details are more specific than our subheading?" At this point (hopefully), some student will suggest, "Maybe, we have added another level to our outline?" And, of course, I (happily) agree. But here's another caution: I have learned that I will need to provide practice, practice, and practice.

When I grade them on their outlines in note taking after I have taught it to them, the entire learning process in my course will have "escalated," and I will have given them a priceless skill. In the end, I save time because they will be able to process information more efficiently because the skill of outlining, with practice, will have become automatic.

This process is further enhanced if I subsequently teach them how to use the outline for my courses on the computer. I constantly carried out this entire process in my courses. Like the longhand one, the outline using the computer must be taught, monitored, practiced, and ultimately graded. Subsequently, the students took great pride in reporting their "outline successes" in other courses.

THE WORLD IS TOO MUCH WITH US

Up to this point, we have specifically discussed and illustrated planning in-class activities and some actions you can take. Now we turn our attention to intrusions upon your classroom teaching that you have no control over and how to prepare for them.

This last section deals primarily with those unexpected events requiring a judgment call. Events like fire drills, although often unannounced, usually have specific routines to follow, and they are often discussed and practiced. The kinds of events we are talking about here are different. No matter how carefully you plan in advance, unexpected instances will either occur in your classroom or will affect it. Among such events are an emergency announcement from the principal's office; a message from the dean about an emergency in your or some student's family; a student suddenly becoming ill; or a kind of catastrophic happening, such as a shooting on the school campus, an incident comparable to 9/11, and the like. But whatever it is, you are in charge, and you need to set an example for your students.

One of the most important things is to recognize that the class session is about to be disrupted, even if it already hasn't been. First, keep your cool, trust your own judgment, and consider who and what can help the students and you in dealing with the situation. So, take charge. Whether you like it or not, *you are in charge and the students want you to be.* Because you are dealing with young adults, treat them as such, and keep them informed if it's an event external to your classroom. If they offer to help, respect their offers and use them if they make sense. Students are often more mature and caring than we give them credit for being. Unless otherwise advised, do not dismiss the class. If the students feel the need to talk about the situation, do so. You represent authority and maturity in this situation, and they will seek your reassurance and insights. If a student is sick, use the intercom if you have one to summon help or have several students take the person to the school nurse or the restroom, stay with the person until professional help arrives, and then report back to you.

If you are the one having the emergency, then complete the class session if at all possible. If that is not possible, and you must leave the room, briefly explain to the students that you have an unexpected problem and give them a meaningful (doable) assignment that won't require you to be there. Ask them to remain in the classroom until the period is over.

As a teacher, you will undoubtedly come up with some of your own forms of preteaching and judgment call activities. The ones we have cited here have worked for us and are designed to help you to prepare for the unexpected in your role as teacher. As you are already finding out, being a teacher is no done deal—and there's a lot more to come.

In the next chapter, we take up classroom management tactics we have found effective over the years. We firmly believe they will help you to be an effective teacher as well. One of these tactics we have already touched on, you being the person in charge.

2

CLASSROOM MANAGEMENT TACTICS

In addition to everything else that being a teacher requires, you also have to be a savvy manager. However, unlike business incentives, the students can neither be paid in money nor can you give them bonuses (when they really perform) or fire them (when they are being awful). You cannot kick them upstairs permanently to be someone else's headache, reassign them to a broom closet, initiate a desk audit, or inundate them with busywork when they fall out of favor. Such management tactics will not do in the classroom. Instead, your managerial skills must take on some subtleties business managers often do not have to cultivate to be successful. At the beginning of the term, your students have two things in common: the subject matter you are teaching (probably required and they may view it as forced labor) and you as their teacher. Thus, it is up to you to manage the class and build the human relationships required for the students to learn and value your subject matter and, with luck and skill, you as a teacher.

So . . . described and illustrated in this chapter are proven management tactics that can assist you in handling diverse student groups, including the disruptive student.

WHO'S IN CHARGE HERE?

You are. Each and every student must pay attention to you if any subject matter learning is to take place. You must gain their attention right from the start. If you don't, they may be learning all right—but it won't be what you have in mind for them. Also, you will be faced with the underprepared, the non-English speakers, and the potential disrupters, and it is bad form to allow them to lurk around in the back seats of the classroom or roam the halls as if they were ghosts. Like the more manageable students, they, too, are members of the class, and you have an obligation to reach and teach them. This means every student's attention must be focused on you *before* you begin *any* class activity. You must establish this routine in the first few minutes of the first class on the first day and then continue to practice it every day throughout the duration of the course, amen. If you don't, you will be wasting valuable class time for the rest of the term, and you are, however inadvertently, downgrading the importance of your subject matter and your role as a teacher.

"All well and good," you say. "But how do I accomplish this?" Here are tactics based on our years of teaching at the elementary, secondary, and postsecondary levels.

- Whenever possible, be the first to arrive in the classroom. If your classes are all in the same room, you have a built-in edge. Be prompt, be pleasant, and greet the students. As part of this greeting, hand each student an agenda. This usually quiets the class down right away. Students want to know what's going on. Maintain this procedure for the rest of the term.
- Stand before beginning the presentation—and remain standing. Avoid sitting or being behind a desk until all students exit. (We say more about this standing business in the next section.) Wait until you have the full attention of everybody present before beginning an activity, whether it is homework checking, test announcements, or starting a presentation. State the class is about to begin. Call the names of a few students who are talking if they don't subside after you have announced that the work of the class is beginning; only rap on a table or desk if most of the students continue to talk or socialize. Use nonverbal cues (pantomime with hand and head gestures) to discourage conversation among students, reading a textbook, or writing notes and thus not paying attention. See Case 2.1.

  If none of these tactics seems to be effective and the whole class is restive, close your notes, stop, wait, and then say to them, "What's going on here? What's distracting you from our class session? This is not your usual style." If nobody volunteers, call on the student who is an instigator, a leader, or one who looks troubled, using that student's name. *Find out.* It may be something completely outside of your class-room (it often is), like a fight on the school grounds, a shooting, or some other incident. But whatever it is, deal with it as humanely and

CASE 2.1

In one of the classes, Introduction to Social Science, 7:00 p.m. to 8:30 p.m., gaining the attention of the thirty-five tired and restless inner-city, minority students in the class was still taking too long, even after the second session and the use of the agenda. Finally, I rapped sharply on the table and said, "Wait a minute. Do you think I don't care whether you learn or not? *I do care* whether you do or not." A brief pause occurred, followed by pin-drop silence. It was the last time I had any problems with this group. Suddenly, they realized somebody cared about them and their learning.

efficiently as possible. Taking time to find out what's wrong and then addressing the situation shows the students you really do care about them, and it will help them to return their attention to the class work at hand.

- Greet latecomers positively and point them to seats in the front if possible. If material has been placed on the chalkboard, leave it there for the latecomers to copy down. If material has been orally presented, instruct them to see their friends after the class about what they have missed. Latecomers who either query you or ask questions of other students waste everyone's time and are disruptive. Also, allowing such interruptions can become habit forming; students begin to feel they can come late and then ask questions. If you have a perennial latecomer, talk with this student about the reason for this behavior. Once in a while, a student really does have a good reason to be late.

- Announce the ground rule of students waiting to be acknowledged before either asking or answering questions at the first class meeting. *Enforce this rule*. It allows you to control and broaden the base of student participation and to avoid domination of the class discussion by one or two students. We'll have more to say about this ground rule later when we arrive at the pedagogical principles.

- Whenever possible, collect homework and other assignments individually from students to add a personal touch. As you collect the assignments or homework, make a brief comment about each particular student's work. Here are a few examples of what we have said: "Beautiful formatting here." "I really like your use of graphics." "What an interesting title!" "Numbering the steps of the problem really helps me to follow what you have done." "No way can I lose your folder with these gorgeous rainbow colors." Also, this is a good time to find out the reasons why a student did not complete the homework or some other assignment, but your inquiry should not embarrass the student. Here are some suggestions for finding out their reasons: "Was there something about the assignment you didn't understand?" "A problem at home that you had to deal with?" "Did you call or talk with one of your colleagues about the work? It's perfectly OK to do so, you know." Depending upon the answer, you can then decide whether to give the student another chance to finish the work, ask another student to help, see the student after class (if possible) or another time, or administer a warning. For example, if a student says, "I had to go to my grandmother's funeral," and this is the fourth time the student has given this reason, you definitely need more than a warning here. (You're probably dealing with a not-too-smooth con artist.) But you should always warn before assigning a penalty, like an F, for the assignment. You must find a way to deal with the situation. Just letting the student off the hook or ignoring the default for an assignment does neither of you any service, and it undermines your authority.

Remember you *are* in charge, and both you and the students must clearly understand that. Otherwise, and we reiterate, the particular learning you have in mind will not be the learning taking place.

STUDENTS HAVE NAMES, TOO

Learning and then calling individual students by their names within the first two weeks of class sends a clear message from you, the teacher: "You matter to me. I care about you—and your learning." Taking the time to learn and use the students' names is important to everyone, but it is particularly critical to the learning of diverse and underprepared students. There are three primary reasons for this practice. First, all too often, these students feel they are simply numbers or nameless faces in a crowd. Being treated as an anonymous nobody is no way to build self-esteem. Second, students have different knowledge levels in any subject matter. Knowing their names allows you to direct specific questions or comments to given students based on your estimate of their knowledge levels. It is a way of personalizing instruction. The third reason relates to your control of the classroom. Calling a student by name who is not paying attention helps to encourage participation in the class learning and it often acts as a deterrent for potentially disruptive behavior. For example, "backbenchers" who are talking to one another and are trying to hide behind their colleagues can easily be called by name, and they will stop talking if you ask one of them a question. It's not so easy with, "Er . . . um, . . . ahem, you in the brown sweater in the back seat there . . ."

"How am I going to do this when I have five classes and 140 students?" you ask. We know of several different ways.

- The cheapest and easiest way that really works is to have each student take a piece of notebook paper, write his or her name in big letters, and display the sign for you so that you can easily read them at a distance. Continue this practice for about two weeks, or until you have learned all of the names.
- Have the students give their names when they ask or answer a question for a few class sessions.
- Another way is to work with the class roster and either memorize these names or call the roll until names and faces match.
- Develop an unobtrusive seating chart with the students' names on it and refer to it in the early days of the course until you have names and faces connected (See Case 2.2).

As a final note here, we want to point out that this tactic of knowing students' names is key to a number of pedagogical principles described in the next two chapters.

YOU'RE ON CENTER STAGE, BABY

You have to manage and hold an audience. Every fine actor does, and so do you as a teacher. Actors are up on their feet a whole lot of the time and you must be, too. So, stand up—you're taller than anybody else when you're standing and the students are sitting—and stay on your feet when you are teaching the whole group. View yourself as being in the starring role and, whether you like it or not, as a teacher, you really are. You must work to keep your audience with you. Be dynamic: not only should you stand but you should move around; change the pitch and tone of your voice; make eye contact and show expression in your face; deliver your message; watch the audience for their response; and be memorable. What all of this is say-

CASE 2.2

An experience one of the authors had with the importance of knowing the students' names came in a conversation with the daughter of a friend who had graduated recently from a university in New York City. Using a fictitious name, the conversation went, as follows:

Author: You know we are having so many problems in education these days. I would like your opinion.

Neena: Tell me. I know I am a good student; I did not learn that much from my teachers; I had to learn most of it myself.

Author: Why is that?

Neena: Teachers come, lecture, and leave.

Author: In your program at the university, do you remember any names of your professors?

Neena: Not really.

Author: Are you sure?

Neena: I remember one.

Author: How come you only remember one?

Neena: This professor knew my name from day one. He always called me by name. I felt like I mattered; I learned a lot. And I worked very hard in his course.

ing is if you act like a spear-carrier, your audience psychologically, if not physically, will soon depart. In other words, if you choose to sit down behind a desk or a table, read aloud from the text, treat your students as nameless passengers in a waiting room, or present your message in a monotone, then you really *are* a spear-carrier in the drama, not a star.

You ask, "How in the world can I be dynamic through five classes?" We answer, "You don't have to do it nonstop. Pace yourself, and use different variations in your teaching." For example, if students are working in small groups, pull up a chair and join them, rotating among the groups to monitor and assist them as needed. If they are taking a test, sit down but be observant. If students are running the discussion, having a debate, or are presenting, then you join the audience as a participant. Don't sit in the front row; sit in the back. You need to monitor their behaviors. But remember: Nikes are not for you. You are not one of the gang.

If there is a desk in the room that cannot be pushed to the side, stand in front or put a chair in front of it. Use the desk for either storage or a staging area. As part of presenting your subject matter, keep the presentation (lecturing) down to five to seven minutes, and then engage students in interactive activities, like a short question-and-discussion session or small-group follow-ups. Then, if need be, you can start presenting again. After all, the Gettysburg Address took about five minutes, and Shakespeare's most famous soliloquies only took about two to three minutes. Be clear, be brief, be to the point, and remember you are an observer as well as a participant. Stop if the students' eyes begin to glaze over, and ask, "Where did I lose you? Somehow, we parted company." They will know; they will tell you. And then you and they can go back to clarify the point. This tactic increases their investment in their own learning and accountability.

We mentioned how you should use a desk if you have one in your classroom. Now consider the other furniture and appointments in your room. If the lecture part of a science class is in the science lab, you're rather stuck. The tables are usually firmly bolted in place, and the stools are about all that can be moved. So try to close the physical distance between yourself and the students by moving around and not always being in front of the class.

In the social sciences and humanities classes, the typical furniture is minimal: chairs with writing arms, often arranged by the cleaning staff in neat rows and well away from the teacher's desk and the chalkboards. The net effect is psychological—if not actual or physical—distance, and it is not conducive to connecting with an audience, which is what your students are. So you need to rearrange the furniture to close the distance and rid yourself of the antiseptic rows. Cleaning staffs are not known for their interior design capabilities, and you may need to talk with them about your requirements if you are lucky enough to have a classroom of your own. Otherwise, you'll have to take up rearrangement of the room yourself. Your students will soon have the message, and they will pitch in to help. This process also helps to create a sense of a special classroom community. Semicircles and clusters are great "de-formalizers": they allow you to see everybody, and everybody can see you. They also eliminate the backbenchers. Do not use a full circle—the visibility to your immediate left and right is reduced, and the distance across from you may be too great if the class is fairly large.

Remember: you are not only the lead actor in this drama, you are also the stage manager.

THE REAL DEAL: MISSION
IMPOSSIBLE—ALMOST

Now we come to a tough patch in the road. From time to time in every subject matter, certain topics will take on the quality of "mission impossible—almost" for both you and the students. For students, it's usually a matter of complete unfamiliarity with or lack of exposure to anything having to do with particular concepts or processes. This situation is particularly prevalent with diverse and underprepared students, and even more so when they come from poverty backgrounds as well. Let us give some examples, using two disciplines, the first from physics (Case 2.3).

CASE 2.3

In a physics course, Planck's hypothesis (quantization of energy or tiny packets of energy as discrete units to which quantum numbers were later assigned) qualifies as a big-time "heavy" concept. Planck's hypothesis is now considered to be one of the main anchors of modern physics, but it sat around without any definite acceptance from the physics community for many years. According to Planck, if f_o is the natural frequency of an oscillator, the next higher energy levels will be hf_o, $2hf_o$, $3hf_o$, . . . and nothing in between. Everybody have that?

For the teacher in a physics course, the problem is to find some way to anchor the hypothesis to students' experiences. In actuality, this problem of anchoring is a tough one here because the hypothesis itself cannot be seen or touched—only its effects can be experienced, just like many terms commonly accepted as useful in psychology, such as cognitive process or the ego, which also cannot be seen or touched—only their effects. Therefore, the task is to explain what a hypothesis is in general (specifically, a formal conjecture about the existence or nonexistence of some phenomenon). Having done that, the next step is to find the means for testing for its theorized existence or nonexistence.

In this regard, I describe the observations of Einstein's photoelectric effects to the students. The observations were not what Einstein and other physicists had expected. Initially, even Einstein could not explain the results of his experiment. After reviewing and checking his data, Einstein discovered that he could actually explain the results if he assumed that energy was quantized, that is, energy is given off in discrete units and not in a continuous flow, exactly the same way Planck had hypothesized. I then explain to the student that the results of the photoelectric effect provided a veri-fication of Planck's hypothesis and led to the familiar concept of a quantum number (energy being quantized).

The students stayed with me without taking a nap because they'd been informed that this concept would be difficult, a familiar analogy was used, and they could connect to the concept of a quantum number.

Now we turn to a different discipline of English, the literature aspect (Case 2.4).

CASE 2.4

The task of understanding meaning in literature, particularly poetry, is complex because of the potential for meaning on more than one level. As a result, poetry is often murky for students. The literal or actual printed words say one thing, but often more is meant than what immediately meets the eye traveling across a page. Poetry, often because of its terseness, can pose special problems to students. These below-surface meanings are often couched in figures of speech, such as metaphors, similes, and person-ification. Here is an example of a seemingly simple poem by Emily Dick-inson.

> Fame is a bee.
> It has a song—
> It has a sting—
> Ah, too, it has a wing.*

In order to understand this poem to its fullest extent, the students must have a grasp of what fame is and what a bee is. Most of them will. If not, the explanation begins here with the literal or surface meaning of this poem's two major elements. The place where the unfamiliarity probably comes is in the combination of the two in the comparison and the minimal way in which it is done. Fame is an abstract concept, but its effects can be pointed out; bee is concrete, something one can see, hear, and feel. The poem takes the characteristics of the bee and equates them with the ef-fects of fame. The overall figure of speech is an extended and very com-pacted metaphor. The task here becomes one of seeing how each of the bee's characteristics can be translated into the characteristics of fame.

Proceed inductively; let the students work through it, including naming people who may exemplify the characteristics of fame. Don't tell them—they'll soon forget. Reassure them that this is not an easy task, but it's one they need to learn how to deal with—and that mastery of it will take practice.

If the students still are having trouble with the task, then switch to a metaphor that is commonly understood, such as everybody knows somebody who is a "drip," and proceed to analyze its particular characteristics and equate them with those of a particular type of individual.

---

*Thomas H. Johnson, ed., *The Complete Poems of Emily Dickinson* (Boston: Little, Brown, 1960), 713.

In explaining the "mission impossible—almost" concepts, you must let the students know that it is OK if they don't understand them the first or second time around. What you accomplish by doing this is to take the major responsibility upon yourself for their learning, making them feel at ease and assuring them that they are not "stupid" if they don't "get it" right away. The students will work to understand the concept or the process involved, and like any actor, you will have communicated something new and important to them, and you will have kept them as an audience.

DO'S AND DIE'S OF NOTE TAKING

A student who takes good notes in a class is likely to flourish in the course; a student who does not is likely to perish from the course. As a teacher, don't assume your students know the techniques of good note taking. Like everything else in school, note taking is a learned behavior. If they don't know, and most likely they don't, then you must teach them. Good note taking is an art, and it is not synonymous with taking dictation. Surprisingly, note taking is an excellent management tactic as well. It channels the learning into the sequences of the particular concepts, processes, supporting facts, and illustrations you want your students to acquire and remember. Also, when the students collectively stop taking notes and you are still presenting, their behavior may be sending one or more signals. For example, you could be talking too fast, you might have digressed from the task at hand, the explanations or examples you are providing have somehow gone wide of the mark, or you overestimate their note-taking capabilities.

Based on our experience, we have identified two types of note taking, largely dependent on the particular disciplines involved. One of them is for math and the sciences; the other is for social sciences and humanities. Here is what we do in our respective courses.

Math and Sciences Outline

For math and the sciences, the current practice is to have the students copy down almost everything written on the chalkboard, as shown in figure 2.1.

Consider the following sample problem from one of my courses in physics.

Problem 3-2[*]: A boy throws a ball upward with an initial speed of 15 m/s. (1) How high does the ball reach? (2) How long will it take to reach the highest point? (3) What is the speed of the ball before hitting the ground? (4) How long did the ball take to reach the ground from the time it left the boy's hand? Neglect the effects of air friction.

Motion Up ($\uparrow$)		Motion Down ($\downarrow$)		Equations/Constants
Given	**Unknown**	**Given**	**Unknown**	
V_i = 15 m/s	$h = d$ = ?	V_i = 0 m/s	V_f = ?	$V = d/t$ .... ①
V_f = 0 m/s	t = ?	d = 11.5 m	T= total time	$V = (V_f + V_i)/2$ ... ②
$a = g$ = -9/8 m/s2		$a = g$ = 9/8 m/s2		$a = (V_f - V_i)/t$ ...... ③
Part 1: The equation to be used in		Part 3: The equation to be used in		$2ad = V_f^2 - V_i^2$ ..... ④
solving for, d, is: $2ad = V_f^2 - V_i^2$		solving for, V_f, is: $2ad = V_f^2 - V_i^2$		$d = V_i t + (1/2) at^2$. ⑤
Substituting the values, we get:		Substituting the values, we get:		g= 32 ft/s^2 or 9.8 m/s^2
$(2)(-9.8)(d) = (0)^2 - (15)^2$		$(2)(9.8)(11.5) = (0)^2 - (V_f)^2$		
-19.6 d = -225		V_f^2 = 225		
d = (-225)/(-19.6)		V_f= $(225)^{1/2}$		
				The equations displayed in this column were already listed on the chalkboard even before we began the solution of the problem. All the symbols had been defined in an earlier session of this class.
d = 11.5 m		V_f =15 m/s		
Part 2: The equation to be used in		Part 4: Total time, T = time taken by		
solving for time, t, is:		the ball going up + time taken by the		
$a = (V_f - V_i)/t$		ball moving downward.		
Substituting values for variables,		T = 1.53 + 1.53		
we get				
-9.8 = (0 – 15)/t		T = 3.06 s		
Therefore t = (-15)/(-9.8)				
t = 1.53 s				

[*]The problem in physics textbooks is that they do not use numeric designations for questions that are asked.

Figure 2.1. Write-up of a Sample Problem in Physics on the Chalkboard by the Teacher

The teaching process used is shown in Case 2.5.

CASE 2.5

1. The first student was asked to read the entire problem slowly, so as to provide an overview of it.

2. A second student was asked to read the first sentence and identify any physical quantities that are either given or unknown. In this case, this student replied, "The only quantity given here is the initial velocity (V_i) of 15 m/s." I then recorded the symbol for the physical quantity and its value on the chalkboard.

3. A third student was asked to read the first question and to identify the unknown physical quantity that is implied. This student replied, "Height, meaning distance, d, is unknown." And I then recorded this information on the chalkboard with a question mark (?) next to the symbol.

4. A fourth student was asked to read the next question and to identify the physical quantity that is unknown here. This student replied, "The unknown is time, t." The same procedure was repeated on the chalkboard.

This process was continued until the class had identified all of the obvious physical quantities, either given or unknown.

5. I then asked the question, "Are there any other physical quantities that have not been given but can be assumed to be given?"

6. A number of other students responded, "The final speed, V_f, is 0 when the ball is moving upward and reaches its highest point." Another well-prepared student commented, "The acceleration, a, that is, g, in this case, is also given." One other student then said, "The initial velocity, V_i, for the downward motion is zero."

As this interchange was going on, I wrote everything that the students provided as either given or unknown on the chalkboard the way it is displayed in figure 2.1.

7. Another student identified the equation that should be used to solve for the first unknown, the distance, d.

8. Another student who was having problems with algebra was asked to assist me with the algebraic part of solving for the unknown vari-

able in order to give that student a "mini-practice" with the algebra in a nonthreatening way.

The last three steps were repeated with the help of six additional students (two students for each step), one of them identifying the equation to be used for the unknown and the other one assisting with the algebraic part of the solution. Approximately half the class of twenty-five students was involved in various steps of solving this particular problem.
Authors' Note: Starting with the first student reading the whole problem to finding the total time involved took approximately twenty minutes. However, writing out the whole problem-solving process for this example in this book took several hours.

You must present a model for the students to follow when writing on the chalkboard. This model includes the organization of the problem into its major parts. Usually, a given problem has more than one part. Within each part, there are steps that must be followed in an appropriate sequence. You label each part and number the steps to the maximum extent possible in a concise and readable manner. Allow time for students to take notes. Then go around the room and monitor the quality of their notes. If the note taking is not adequate, find out why. If most students are having a problem, first look at yourself. How good is your model? If your model is really good, then you look at what the students are doing. If most of the students are having difficulties, stop right there and teach note taking. If only a few students are having problems, instruct them on the importance of following the model on the chalkboard. Monitor these students continuously and provide additional help, calling attention to the sequence involved. Numbering the steps in the sequence will help them and you in solving the problem during class and later in their practicing the problem on their own.

Social Sciences Outline

The other note-taking model is for the social sciences and the humanities. Case 2.6 demonstrates an example taken from psychology that covers the id, ego, and superego of Freud. Unlike the sciences, you as a social science teacher might not use the chalkboard that much. More will be done with presentation, followed by discussion or questions and answers. Often there is no clear-cut model for the students to follow. You need to tell them

CASE 2.6

In presenting the outline, I note that it will be in three levels. In this case, it will be Sigmund Freud's topography of personality, which is like a map of the structure of the human personality. I also point out we will eventually add other major parts to the outline, so we will have his full conception. However, today the focus will be on the topography.

1. Freud's Topographical Map of an Individual's Personality [General Category]
    1.1. Id [Subcategory]
        1.1.1. An undifferentiated entity solely in pursuit of pleasure [Identifying characteristic]
        1.1.2. Basic energy source
    1.2. Ego
        1.2.1. Energy from the Id
        1.2.2. "Mediator" between the id (pleasure-seeking) and the superego (pain-avoiding) aspects of the personality
        1.2.3. Rational; tied to language functions
    1.3. Superego
        1.3.1. Energy from the id
        1.3.2. Internalization of society's moral code via parenting figures in the environment
        1.3.3. Parallel to conscience/pain
2. Freud's Dynamics of Personality in Order of Development (Subsequently, this level one heading will also be presented after the topographical one is discussed and examples are presented.)

they need to take notes in an outline form and explain to them that your presentation is organized that way. You must emphasize the important points that students must learn, including salient supporting information and examples. In addition, don't talk too fast. If your speaking sounds slow to you, it's probably about right for the class. Remember the old saying, "Slow and easy gets you there." Then you must monitor students' note taking. If their note taking is terrible in general, which is typical in the social sciences and humanities, stop right there. The time has come to teach note taking in an outline form right now. You can enforce their learning of note taking by collecting and grading their notes. Also, have students double-space their notes for clarity of review and for being able to insert information.

Establishing the routine of practicing, monitoring, and even grading students' outlines will ensure the habituation of an extremely important study skill in the long term and an improvement in student performance in your class in the short term.

YOU ARE TEACHING—NOT THE BOOK

Let us describe two scenarios. In the first one, we refer to this kind of teacher in the third person here because we know it will *not* be you.

This teacher walks in and nods to the students. The class comes to order, the teacher opens the book to page ___, and the students do the same. The teacher lectures or reads from the book. Students initially follow along in the book or read ahead, and some of them may or may not ask related questions. Some students will start to doze off. The teacher covers about half to two-thirds of the chapter and assigns the rest of the chapter for students to read, including homework, while the bell is ringing. The students depart. What an exhilarating experience! Obviously, the book has become the teacher (Take another look at Case 2.2).

If this is the scenario in this teacher's classroom, why is the school shelling out money? Just buying the particular book for the students should be enough. There is no need to waste money on a robot.

Let us describe another kind of scenario. Hopefully, this one will be yours, so we use the second person here.

You walk in and greet students by name. You pass out the agenda and collect any homework assignment individually from each student if time permits (a chance to recognize each student). Then you ask for questions on the previous session or on the progress of an assignment. You answer the questions and review the previous session briefly with the students assisting in review when appropriate. (The principle here is a stitch in time saves nine.) You and the students set the textbook aside and follow the agenda that is arranged to allow for your short presentations followed by questions, discussion, and clarifications. You constantly monitor the incoming nonverbal behaviors of students and act to keep the students alive and focused on the subject matter at hand rather than turning them into dozers, fidgeters, and talkers. Lastly, you discuss and assign homework only on the topics covered during the class period and do so before the bell rings. You never assign new and unfamiliar topics for reading that you know your students perceive as difficult.

If the second scenario is what is occurring in your classroom, then you are teaching and earning every nickel of your pay.

Regarding homework, you should give students a break once in a while and not assign any—thereby winning the teacher-of-the-year award—at least for twenty-four hours. When assignments are made, you should keep in mind that length is not synonymous with strength. In this context, Kauchak and Eggen note,

> Many homework *assignments are excessive*. If the presentation and guided practice phases are properly executed, students should be able to complete their assignments quickly and effectively. When this happens, performance improves and motivation increases. Researchers have also found that in addition to amount, the frequency of homework is important; for example, 10 problems every night is more effective than 50 once a week. Students should expect homework as one of their classroom routines, and it should be collected, scored, and returned.[1]

In our cases, we have found that assigning too much is overwhelming and discourages many students from doing anything at all. Assigning homework sparingly and making certain that everyone can perform, and then collecting it and scoring it faithfully have done wonders in terms of students actually taking an interest in doing the homework. Sometimes, we utilize group collaboration if it is going to benefit students. It is particularly valuable with minority and underprepared students because it enables them to pool their strengths and find "safety in numbers." If someone doesn't perform, we find out the reasons and provide appropriate assistance right away. The rule here is: use homework to reinforce, never to introduce. This point is also made by Kauchak and Eggen when they note, "Seatwork and homework do not teach; they reinforce earlier learning."[2]

EQUAL STUDENT PARTICIPATION—AN OVERLOOKED STUDENT CIVIL RIGHT

Equal student participation in a class sounds good, doesn't it? But it is more than a slogan. It really is a student right to have an equal chance to participate and to contribute. For diverse populations, it is critical. All too often, such students have experienced violations of civil rights, so your practicing a "civil right" in the classroom may be a refreshing new experience for them. For us, this term means that over the course of the term, each student actually will have been recognized and will have contributed about the same number of times for questions, answers, and discussion as every other student. We don't want to imply that this form of equal participation has to be achieved in each and every class session because the tasks of a given session vary, but equal participation needs to be realized over a period of several class sessions, and it must be very obvious to students. Now, how do you achieve equal student participation in your class?

First, as a teacher, you must assume your students can, want to, and will learn what you have to teach them, even when some of them look turned off, "out to lunch," or terrified at the beginning. "How can I make every student learn my subject matter in my class?" you ask. Many times, this is easier said than done.

Let us describe the approaches that do work and explain why they work. Some are direct, as in calling the students by name; others are indirect, as in assuming every student can learn.

- On day one of the class, let students know, "I may be teaching a subject matter that is required and not of much interest personally to every one of you, but we are in it together, and each one of us has a role to play." This sends a message that you have some understanding about their feelings, often none too positive, toward this particular subject matter, and it is the beginning of setting the students at ease.

- If some students are not learning, say to them, "You're having trouble learning this subject matter. I know you are trying, and you do have to take this course, so I think I need to take a look at my teaching because we are partners in this course together. You are signaling to me that I have lost you. What happened?" Your candor will encourage students to tell you where you have lost them, where they are having trouble without feeling stupid. Discuss the situation with them. Then follow up by commenting on their strengths: "You are showing up, you are taking notes, and you are paying attention." Focusing on their strengths, including their insights into the problem, requires you to stay focused on how to help them instead of jumping to the conclusion (even if unsaid): "You, the students, are not prepared and if you are not learning, then it's your fault." The big thing here is to communicate to the students positively, avoid the easy cop-out of being negative, and refrain from soothing your own ego by playing assorted variations on the students' weaknesses. Although it is easier to blame someone else than it is to look at one's own flaws, sometimes it's necessary.

- Make the students feel they are real people. Learn their names and use their names in greeting them, asking questions, and praising a response or project. What you accomplish through this practice is to show you care, it makes them feel they're important, and you engage their attention. The net effect is they will not only gradually become more positive toward you and the class but they are likely to become active learners as well.

- Use group process in solving problems, working on assignments, even taking tests you have prepared. With this last point, tests—particularly yours—should be designed to show where you need to reteach as well as how well the students have learned the material. Involve both swifties and strugglers in the same group. Sometimes the swifties can put the points across to their colleagues better than you can.

- You must find a way to deal with the disrupters. With a student who engages in disruptive behavior, such as standing up and looking out a window, deliberately dropping books and other materials on the floor, elaborately yawning or shaking a watch in seeming disbelief at the slow passage of time, starting to engage in grooming or putting on make-up, stop whatever you are doing. Call the person by name, and instruct him or her to remain for a few minutes after you dismiss the class. It may be worth dismissing the class a few minutes early if you have another class immediately following this one. If at all possible, find out what the problem is, and point out this behavior is interfering with the learning of other students and their right to learn. If this student is singularly underprepared, try to find a resource within the school for assistance—any reading or math tutoring service available, an ESL resource person, counselor, assistant principal, even another student who seems to be a good friend—for insights into the problem. *Above all, take action, and do so in private.*

- Remember, always, that you have an entire class to teach—not just a few seemingly more able students or the average ones. In order to reach the entire class, make certain students know that they must be recognized by you by name before speaking (asking or answering a question, and commenting, giving an opinion, or narrating experiences). This practice will allow you maintain control of the class and ensure a widespread student participation in the class sessions.

Practicing these management tactics consistently will give you control of the classroom. Without control, teaching is impossible. Your own teaching will be enhanced if you can observe an experienced teacher using these techniques. Having come this far, you should be realizing that effective teaching is no simple recipe-following matter—if indeed you ever thought it was. Take a deserved break, and then read on.

NOTES

1. D. P. Kauchak and P. D. Eggen, *Learning and Teaching* (New York: Allyn and Bacon, 2003), 375.

2. Kauchak and Eggen, *Learning and Teaching*, 375.

3

BASIC TEACHING PRINCIPLES

In the first two chapters, we shared with you critical planning activities and management tactics and techniques to facilitate your teaching. Essential as these practices are to effective teaching, they are not the crux of the teaching process. We have placed them in this order because they are easier to understand, can be observed directly, and are more readily acquired than the teaching principles.

In this chapter, we present what we have come to view as the four most basic teaching principles in the teaching repertory: anchoring, deductive vs. inductive learning, accelerate slowly, and lastly, practice, practice, and practice = mastery. Each principle is defined, discussed, and illustrated. The combined use of these principles is demonstrated in two teaching dialogues in the final part of the chapter since many teaching principles and management tactics come into play simultaneously in the course of a teaching session. One of the more important teaching principles is anchoring. So we begin this chapter with this particular teaching principle.

ANCHORING—TYING NEW CONCEPTS TO FAMILIAR EXPERIENCES OF YOUR STUDENTS

High school or entering freshmen college students actually bring vast collections of knowledge with them into any classroom they enter. The trick for you as a teacher is to tap into this knowledge base in a selective way—in other words, to tie concepts and processes of what you are teaching to what they already know. This is the teaching principle of anchoring. Anchoring is a special case of a broader principle known as inductive learning, and its most critical characteristic is finding something in the students' experiences that ties to the unfamiliar or only minimally understood concepts, terms, or processes they are expected to learn in your courses. In the following discussion, we use the word *construct* to represent any concept, process, term, or definition.

Here's why this teaching principle is so important. First, you gain the students' attention and they realize they have something to contribute. Second, they will have a better understanding of the construct. As a result, they will remember the construct and they will have a familiar connection to it. Third, they are likely to be able to apply or use the construct more easily in other situations or problems. If this principle is consistently applied, students will feel learning your subject matter is important because they are contributing to their own learning and not confined to only absorbing. More importantly, they will be finding out that the course is doable. Along the way, they will become more active learners.

Let us illustrate the application of the anchoring principle with several examples (See Case 3.1).

Now let us examine another example in physics (See Case 3.2). Frictional force in a typical physics course is defined as $f = \mu N$, where f is the force of friction, μ is the coefficient of friction, and N is the normal force. As soon as this equation is written, students dutifully copy all the information

---

CASE 3.1

In a typical math course at the eleventh- or twelfth-grade level, the math teacher will teach trigonometric functions (like sine and cosine) and will use a right-angled triangle in explaining them. All these concepts are totally abstract and often can elicit a "so what" or "I can't do this" attitude on the part of students. However, you will knock their socks off if you tell them that these functions are used in computing the number of yards a quarterback wants to cover in a single pass without being intercepted. Now, to the best of our knowledge, Joe Montana, Donovan McNabb, and other great quarterbacks have not carried calculators with them in preparation for their passing, but intuition, feel, and practice have allowed them to apply these sine and cosine functions with great success. If you carefully study a quarterback's body movement and preparatory throwing actions as he drops back to pass, you will see him setting up to apply these functions. After all, the angle for a "Hail Mary" is very different from that of a quick screen pass, and a quarterback most assuredly knows the difference.

down. Next, they take on a glazed look and are usually afraid to ask for clarification of the definition or about its usefulness. Hopelessness followed by self-protective disinterest soon sets in. Often a teacher will ignore these student distress signals and will go on to overwhelm them in the use of this equation. The students will all too often tune it out, memorize it, and soon forget it.

However, if this definition is anchored to the students' experiences, they are much more likely to remember it for a long time. In the anchoring example that follows, it shows the resourcefulness of one of the authors in sidestepping a student's response that, while actually appropriate, would have produced a laugh and might have derailed the class session as a whole.

CASE 3.2

Teacher	(*open question to class*) Can anyone provide an example of friction being useful and another example where it is undesirable?
Student₁	I have a dirty mind: I do know the answer, but I am not going to say.
Teacher	(*grinned a little, acknowledged the student's unspoken answer, and quickly focused on another student*)
Student₂	With a car engine, we put in oil to reduce friction (*answering the undesirable part of the question*).
Teacher	Well done, but what about giving us an example where friction is desirable? (*A long silence*)
Teacher	Well, how about this. Can you stop a car on ice?
Students	No, it will slide, slip.
Teacher	Now, can you tell where friction is desirable?
Students	Of course, we can. You need lots of friction to stop the car.
Teacher	You mean between the tires and the road.
Students	Yes.
Teacher	So the frictional force is between two surfaces—in this case, between the tires and the road.

Now, we shift out of the sciences into the social sciences with an example taken from an introductory social statistics/measurement course (Case 3.3). In this example, the topic at hand is scales of measurement and a preliminary introduction to what you can and cannot do with them.

The four scales of measurement are important in statistics and testing because they determine what kinds of methods or techniques can be used in ascertaining the main patterns of meaning from a set of quantitatively reported data (numbers). In other words, the same number can convey different meanings. It depends on how it's used. The idea of a two or a three or a four having different meanings assigned to them is often difficult for students to grasp—mathematics is hard enough for them without the numbers themselves turning out to be shifty, as is the case with the four measurement scales in social science statistics (See Case 3.3).

CASE 3.3

I often begin this discussion by asking what 4 means to them. Someone will say, "the number of items in a group, like people, or things" (ratio scale). Another might say, "A very low car license plate number in D.C." (nominal scale). I ask for any other meanings. Someone else adds, "A bad score on a quiz having 30 items" (interval scale) and laughs a little. "True enough," I say. Then I ask, "How about contestants in a beauty pageant, like the Cherry Blossom Festival here in D.C.?" (ordinal scale). The students laugh a little, with one commenting, "I don't think coming in fourth is exactly terrific." Another student says, "Well, how about four being two squared?" (ratio scale again). "All good examples of the different meanings that can be assigned to the number 4, and indeed of any number," I comment, having written all the examples on the chalkboard.

Then I state, right now we are using numbers for identification or categorizing purposes. "Does it make any sense if we add the numbers of four license plates together?" The students laugh and say, "No." I agree, and ask, "Then what do we have them for?" "So the cops can get you for speeding or boot your car if you haven't paid your tickets." "True enough, but how do they know?" I ask. "Because each car has a different license plate, and there's a record of every license plate on the computer at the Department of Motor Vehicles, so they know who it is. Believe me, I know," another student responds. I ask, "What other examples of numbers like this can you think of?" Various students respond, "Social Security numbers, credit card numbers, lottery tickets, . . ."

From this point, I can explain that numbers used here are for identification purposes and are specifically used to differentiate one number or category from another. In statistical work, we refer to them as belonging to the nominal scale; they deal with categories only. In the social sciences, categories, such as males and females or Republicans and Democrats, are often of interest, and there are some statistical techniques, like chi square (X^2), for dealing with them. The process of anchoring then repeats itself for the remaining three scales. In presenting the remaining three scales, I will go back to the examples the students have given and begin the discussion from there.

A final reason for using anchoring and for presenting it first is because it is so important to be able to communicate effectively and immediately with underprepared and diverse student populations. All too often, such students are not used to succeeding.

DEDUCTIVE VS. INDUCTIVE LEARNING

Deductive learning may be viewed as the teacher first giving a definition of a concept or important term. Then the teacher often illustrates the concept with a concrete example and hopefully points out the salient characteristics of the concept contained in the example. In many cases, the teacher moves on, although students may be asked sometimes to give other appropriate examples. All too often, the teacher moves on before the students have really grasped or internalized the concepts. Too often, this approach results in students as passive learners. Students are not sure, and they are afraid to ask questions for fear of looking stupid—so they remain silent, and the teacher moves on. Let us illustrate this first by an example in a physics course (Case 3.4).

CASE 3.4

The teacher introduces the term *speed*, defines it as distance/time, provides the units as miles per hour (MPH), and illustrates it by stating that your speed on a typical highway could be 55 MPH. The teacher then asks the question, "Does everybody understand?" Each student looks around to see if anyone else is going to ask for clarification or another example. This question is a champion put-down. No student wants to look like a dummy in front of peers or the teacher. Without waiting for an answer from students or checking for nonverbal cues of puzzlement, blankness, or glazed eyes, the teacher introduces the next term in that chapter. Of course, the students will forget this definition within several days, maybe in a few minutes. And worse, at least some of them are developing an edgy feeling about being successful in the course as well.

The social sciences can go this example one better (Case 3.5).

CASE 3.5

The teacher introduces the concept of culture and then defines it as "'the distinctive way of life of a group of people,' like that of America or Japan." Then the teacher notes that included in culture are such social institutions as language, family structures, values, type of government, and economic system. The students dutifully write down the definition and the examples. Even if the teacher asks for any questions, the definition and examples are so general the students do not know where to start. A golden opportunity is forfeited to talk about how cultures evolve in response to differing geographic and climatic challenges and situations. Also forfeited is why all of us are immersed in one culture or another or are trying to bestride more than one culture simultaneously, as is the case with recent immigrants and students from poverty backgrounds. The concept of culture is reduced to an abstract definition, having little direct meaning to the students.

In our opinion, deductive learning should be minimized or not used at all in the beginning of any introductory course and particularly with diverse and/or underprepared student populations. These populations often lack the necessary background knowledge to bring to the concept, fail to see the relevance of their own experiences to the concept, and are inexperienced in handling abstraction. (Their own lives are generally filled with the concrete and immediate needs associated with survival.) Finally, they may lack the vocabulary necessary for dealing effectively with the concept and its application. As a result, these students tune out because the presentation really is beyond their grasp. Their defense will be that the class is boring, and they will learn to dread the class instead of learning the subject matter.

Inductive learning proceeds in a reverse fashion. Here, the concept or term is mentioned, and the students are questioned as to their understanding of it or asked to give examples. From the examples and partial understanding, a clear definition of the concept or term is derived.

Now let us return to speed and see how this concept is handled in inductive learning (See Case 3.6).

Now we return to the definition of culture in order to illustrate how the same concept is handled in an inductive learning approach (See Case 3.7).

CASE 3.6

Teacher	Now, I am on item #3 on the agenda, and the term that needs defining is speed. Let us consider Washington, D.C. (DC) and New York City (NYC) as two cities for the sake of explanation. How long does it take you to go from DC to NYC?
Student₁	Five hours.
Teacher	Everybody agrees?
Students	OK. That sounds reasonable.
Teacher	Here, we are talking about the physical quantity of time. Now, let me ask you another question. How fast were you driving?
Student₂	Anywhere from stop to 80 MPH.
Student₃	Usually about 55 MPH—my average speed (*another physical quantity*).
Teacher	OK. How far is NYC from DC? (*a third physical quantity, distance, is introduced without students being aware of its label*)
Students	About 200–250 miles depending upon where someone lives.
Teacher	What are the different physical quantities we have talked about?
Students	(pause) Speed, . . . Distance, . . . Time, . . . Direction—in this case, north MPH
Teacher	We have five answers here. Are they all physical quantities?
Student₄	MPH is a unit of speed—not a physical quantity by itself.
Student₅	I am not too sure, but I don't think direction is really a physical quantity.
Teacher	What do the rest of you think?
Students	We are not too sure either, but what the other students said sounds right.
Teacher	They are right. Let me clarify. Direction is used to distinguish between a scalar and a vector quantity as learned earlier. Now, suppose the distance is actually 200 miles and it took you four hours to get to NYC. What is your average speed?
Students	50 MPH.
Teacher	How did you get this answer?
Students	We divided 200 by 4.
Teacher	OK. Now, can you give me a definition of speed?
Students	Sure. Speed = distance/time

CASE 3.7

I begin with asking the students what their idea of culture is. A typical response is, "going to an art museum or a concert." I answer, "Yes, that's part of it: the arts are important." Then I ask, "Suppose you were born and are living in Mexico or Spain, what language would you be speaking?" Several students answer, "Spanish." I then ask, if you were Syrian or Jordanian, what language would you be speaking then?" "Arabic," said one female student. "I'm from Egypt; Arabic is my first language." "Good," I say. "One of the essential elements of a culture is its language. What else might culture include?"

The discussion continues with the students contributing their ideas, among which are clothing styles, values, types of government, technology, family arrangements, religion, and so on. All of their contributions are building toward and deepening their grasp of culture as an all-embracing concept. Finally, a student who has been quietly listening to the discussion comments, "We are all living in a culture; it's all around us. We can't escape it."

I comment, "You are right. Culture is the distinctive way of life for an identifiable group of people. It may be huge, like India or China, or very small, like a tribe of hunter-gatherers in the rain forest of the Amazon, but it will always have the same essential elements that its members understand and pass on. And when you leave one culture and enter another one that is new to you, you find yourself having to make all kinds of adjustments to the new one." Some of the students nod in agreement, and one more outspoken one says, "And it's not easy, I tell you!"

To someone who is unfamiliar with these teaching techniques, this type of interchange may seem long and drawn out. In actuality, writing it all out does take time, but carrying it out takes just a few minutes. Most importantly, the students have not only acquired an accurate initial understanding of the concept but they will retain the concept for a long time and will be active partners in their learning.

The inductive approach has at least one additional advantage. It allows the teacher and sometimes a student to elaborate on and to clarify the meaning of a new use of a common term. The previous example in physics of inductive learning clearly demonstrates where both the teacher—and, on this occasion, the students as well—elaborated and clarified the critical points regarding units of physical quantities. In the social science example, the teacher and the students gradually built a concept of culture, drawing and capitalizing upon the students' diverse experiences. In subsequent class sessions, the concept will be elaborated on and applied further to everyday situations.

ACCELERATE SLOWLY

In our experiences in the teaching of sociology, social research, social statistics, physics, math, and computer science, we have determined critical elements that frustrate and slow down the classes in learning the course content. For the sciences, including social statistics, it is the fear of math and/or the students' inability to carry out basic algebraic steps that constitute real problems. Another problem is tapping the relevant experiences they have had. For example, the class is slowed down a great deal when students keep on asking how the teacher went from step A to step C in spite of having all the steps written on the chalkboard. If these concerns are not addressed, the students are constantly embarrassed and become very frustrated. Soon, they will not ask at all. At the beginning of the course in social statistics, the fear of having to use math is often so extreme that the students cannot even hear what the teacher has to say.

In English, it is the structure of the language itself.

In non-math-related courses serving diverse students, instruction usually is slowed down because of one or more of the following factors: poor organizational ability, weak reading and writing skills, shaky language proficiency, or a diversity of experience that is not geared to the American audience or experience. The task in the social sciences then is to involve these students immediately on day one of the course because they are going to have to work much harder than well-prepared students to be successful. For example, a commonly used textbook for an introductory social science course is daunting enough just to look at the print size and the number of pages involved. That's just for openers.

Chapter 1 starts right out with an abstract definition of scientific knowledge, followed by introducing the concept of the disciplines of the social sciences as a system of rules with regard to seeking, processing, and reporting information. Next comes a highly compact and abstract comparison between social science and science and the search for a unified theory comparable to that proposed for physics. In turn, a description follows of the scientific method and a comparison of that with its application to the social sciences, and we are only at midpoint in the chapter. And this is the introductory course! This is surely a prescription for diverse students to fail early and avoid the rush.

Now the question arises as to how we, the authors of this book, solve these problems with these kinds of students. At the heart of the solution in its simplest form are, in addition to anchoring and the inductive approach previously described, three simple, but important and quite often overlooked, teaching guidelines. First, start where the learner *really* is and not where you as the teacher or the author(s) of the book thinks the student should be. In the social sciences, this means finding a way to link the students' experiences to the subject matter of the course. Often this will involve an analogy of some sort, but it must be accurate. This practice is particularly important if there is a departmental examination involved.

Second, front-load the course with the most essential elements needed to overcome the immediately observable critical deficiencies, even if it means walking the students through the specialized meanings of seemingly familiar words as well as the pronunciation of difficult or brand new words. In the case of the social sciences, take the time to show them how to read the material in a focused way, such as reading the introductory and concluding paragraphs first to check on where the main emphases of the chapter are. Then have the students do a quick scan to note what terms and definitions are bold-faced or italicized and then repeated in a glossary, since they are likely to appear on a test. Underscore that a one-time reading of a chapter, even when they know where the emphases are, won't begin to be enough to understand and remember the key points—and particularly so if the television set is on. Warn the students about the importance of certain concepts, and assure them that you will work with them to develop the necessary understanding of these concepts.

Third, take the time to explain and illustrate clearly, using the anchoring and inductive techniques. Even though it may seem time-consuming, drawing upon the students' experiences and fitting them into the new content pays off in terms of their understanding of it and their confidence in being able to learn. And the students feel that what they know is valuable. When appropriately used, the analogy is an instance of both these techniques in action. When it is not, the students are derailed into a quagmire. Gradually, you can pick up steam with a little help from the deductive approach, but only when you are at least one-third of the way through the course. Taken together, these three guidelines add up to the "accelerate slowly" principle.

Two examples follow that illustrate the set of guidelines in action. The first is taken from the introductory course in social science, first day of the class, with the introductory chapter mentioned previously.

The second example is from part two of an introductory physics course (See Case 3.8/3.9).

CASE 3.8

On opening day of the introductory social science course, after greeting students, having them print their names in large print, and walking them through the syllabus, I ask if anybody has looked at the introductory chapter of the textbook. Usually, one or two students will nod cautiously, but with a marked lack of enthusiasm. "Awful, isn't it?" I ask. And they cautiously agree, not knowing quite what to expect, but my question has startled them.

I pause, and then I tell them, "You really have the experience to understand this stuff—even this horrific first chapter. This chapter talks about social science as a system of rules. We'll tackle the scientific method in a little while. Actually, you know all about rules. You've been living with them most of your lives. Let's take one system of rules—sounds fancy, doesn't it? But most of you know how to drive a car, yes?" The class nods. "OK," I say. "Let's take driving. What do you do when a light turns red as you are approaching an intersection?" A couple of students variously comment, "You're supposed to stop." "Stop." "Hit the brakes."

I ask the other students, "Do you agree?" Everybody does. Then I ask, "What happens when somebody doesn't stop, and just goes right on through?" By this time, the class is into it, and there's a show of hands and commentary. Among the answers are: "You can hit somebody—and that's trouble—big time." "People get mad and blow their horns at you." "You might get caught and get a big fat ticket." The conversation proceeds a little, incorporating what a green light means. What the behaviors of the drivers should be in terms of green and red lights are both rules. These particular rules are a part of the rules and regulations for driving that are analogous to the social sciences as a system of rules, too.

CASE 3.9

Once again, from the experience of many years of teaching, I have made a list of topics in algebra that are used *every day* throughout the course. Those topics include scientific notation, powers of ten in simple and complex situations, simple algebraic equations, and cross-multiplication. I front-loaded the presentation of these topics on day one of the course. The only homework assigned was on these topics. I spent time explaining when a question was asked even with regard to the most rudimentary math concept, powers of ten, how I traveled from step A to step C in solving a physics problem. Keep in mind that the concept of powers of ten is subsidiary to the solution of the problem.

This situation of the students asking these basic questions and then my explaining occurs about every ten minutes during a class period at the beginning of the course. By the middle of the semester, some colleagues might view me as being "behind" a day or two. By this time, the frequency of the "how" questions ("How do I go from step A to step C?") decreases and explaining the basic math concepts is no longer needed. As a result, I can begin to use some features of the deductive method and can accelerate the course. At the end of the course, every student was still there in my class, nobody was failing, and the course content had been fully covered. In contrast, in my colleagues' courses, around 80 percent of the students had dropped out.

PRACTICE, PRACTICE, AND PRACTICE = MASTERY

Understanding a concept, a process, or a skill is necessary but insufficient for mastery and subsequent application. Basic skills, such as the multiplication tables in math, first letter capitalization of the first word in a sentence, and keyboarding in computer usage must be practiced until such time as they become automatic and can be recalled instantly for use without having to think about them. In point of fact, basic skills can be expanded to include computation, reading, and nonfictional writing. Other authors have referred to this kind of mastery as "overlearning" and "automaticity." "Mastery of basic skills allow[s] us to plug in the skills while we perform other cognitive operations."[1] Kauchak and Eggen cite previous research and conclude, "This is a strong argument for overlearning. Our available working memory is limited and automatized skills free memory space that can be devoted to more complex tasks."[2]

Like these authors, we have found overlearning or mastery of basic skills contributes to students' success in their course work. Let us illustrate this key principle using two situations in a typical introductory physics course and a third example drawn from a social science course (See Cases 3.10, 3.11, and 3.12).

CASE 3.10

In any single day, students from time to time draw a blank on something they should be familiar with and they should have understood. Instead, they surprise you and say, "I just don't get it." As a teacher, I know these students should have understood the steps outlined. What to do? Instead of taking valuable class time, I ask these students to write out the steps at least three times exactly as they appear on the chalkboard when the students return home. I also commented, "If the steps are still unclear to you by the time of the next class, I will go over the problem again." When the students returned, I immediately ask, "Are the steps still unclear?" Smilingly, the students report, "No sir, I figured it out." "I was just having a bad day." "I guess I was out to lunch in the last class." This kind of practice typically is used for each class session.

CASE 3.11

When I know a problem is important for students to develop mastery but it is difficult, I will explain and then solve the problem, writing every step on the chalkboard. I know students have understood the problem, but have not mastered it. I will ask the entire class to write out only that particular problem four or five times. In order to underscore the importance of the problem and to ensure full student participation, I tell the students they will see this problem again, presumably on a test. The sheer practice with the problem will ensure they can solve it fully when it appears on the next test with the numbers changed and language somewhat modified.

The students are also encouraged to consult with one another. As a student develops an increasingly clearer understanding of this particular problem, he or she often can explain it to other students. The sheer familiarity with the problem often leads to increased insight into it. They begin to have a real feel for it. Soon they are able to complete the task successfully because the task has become familiar, doable, and manageable, and so they have mastered it.

Why does repetition or practice work? Let us use an analogy to sports. Many people watch basketball games, and they are very familiar with the rules and a lot of the plays. Can they actually become players themselves just by knowing the rules and recognizing the plays? The answer is no. Anyone who wants to play must be on the court and practice and practice and practice. In the example above, a student who can observe the presentation, take notes, and solve the problem once with supervision is like the spectator at the basketball game. If this student wants to do well in the course, the problem solution must be practiced again and again until this student becomes proficient, just as the basketball player must do. Case 3.11 illustrates this.

Let us illustrate the practice-mastery point further by taking an example from a social science course (Case 3.12). In this case, the skills involved are note taking in an outline form after having discovered that the students' note-taking skills ranged from shaky to nonexistent on one of the first presentations of the semester.

The principles described in this chapter along with some of the management tactics are illustrated in the two dialogues that follow: the first one is in English, and the second one is in computer science.

CASE 3.12

I facilitated the practice of these skills by organizing and presenting my next presentation in an outline form that was short. I also told the students I would use a three-level outline, explained what this meant, and demonstrated the first several parts on the chalkboard. During the presentation, I walked around the classroom to see if they were following the outline form. After the presentation, I immediately collected each student's notes to make certain the notes had been taken and their outlines paralleled mine. In cases where their outlines did not, I showed the students my outline, explained again the levels of the outline, and then had them redo their own outlines, using a double-spacing format. I then announced that I would be grading their notes until further notice.

In subsequent class sessions, I collected their notes and graded them, including making corrections and comments. Not surprisingly, the class participation was 100 percent. After all, they were being graded, and six weeks later, the class had habituated the skills, and students were reporting their studying for quizzes had become more systematic. By the end of the semester, various students reported back to me that they were using their new note-taking skills successfully for other courses.

Dialogue: Lesson on Using a Comma in English Nonfiction Writing

The *comma* is for both native English-speaking and non-native English-speaking people the most difficult punctuation mark to work with. It has a tendency to show up when least expected in a sentence, to be added somewhere in a sentence because the writer thinks that one ought to go there, and to be used because the writer has not used one for a while and now thinks that he or she should. When these instances occur, the sentence has a tendency to self-destruct. Comma usage is not that difficult in writing fiction (e.g., novels, plays, poetry) where commas, periods, and semicolons are used in ways that are not appropriate in nonfiction writing. In nonfiction writing (e.g., essays, reports, memoranda, proposals), it has six major uses: (1) with introductory phrases, (2) with introductory clauses, (3) with coordinating conjunctions, (4) with items in a series, (5) with nonrestrictive clauses and phrases (sentence fillers), and (6) with special case conjunctions—for example, however, hence, therefore.

Within this lesson, the focus is on the use of commas following a dependent clause as a lead-in to the independent clause and in the joining of two independent clauses with a coordinating conjunction intervening. Part of a student's paper will be used as the basis for the discussion. This lesson presents a positive approach to the use of commas. It does not deal with the negative, the misplaced or misused comma. Rather, it is essentially dealing with comma omissions. When beginning with grammar and punctuation rules, the students need to see correct usage and build a knowledge base of such usage. Later, if the teacher wishes to do so, he or she may present examples of correct and incorrect usage for reinforcement and review.

For the purposes of this lesson, the following assumptions are made:

- The students know the differences between an independent clause (complete sentence on its own) and a dependent clause (a sentence fragment). They are aware of the signaler words indicating the start of a dependent clause (e.g., because, since, although, if, after, when, before).
- The students are familiar with coordinating conjunctions (i.e., and, but, or, nor) and understand that they generally join equals together (complete sentences). The term *equals* here means in terms of the parts of the sentences.
- The students are familiar with the use of the period and the question mark.

In dialogue 3.1, which deals with English, and the dialogues that follow, when a particular teaching principle or management tactic is first being practiced, it is shown in the right-hand column, meaning that this principle or tactic will be employed for the rest of the dialogue. In this instance, the management tactics of "gaining and maintaining every student's attention," "calling every student by name," and "allowing adequate student response time" will be used concurrently throughout the dialogue. Also occurring at the same time will be "anchoring," "equal participation," and "inductive learning." While the guideline of "using the differential knowledge base of students" is actually being employed right from the start, its presence becomes obvious about midway through the dialogue as the questions being directed to the students clearly reflect an increasing level of difficulty. The first column identifies the different students contributing to the dialogue with the teacher and shows the interaction between them and the subject matter content. The second column presents the teaching principles and management tactics that are being used in the lesson excerpt; teaching principles are identified by a star (*), management tactics are represented by a box (■).

A teacher must provide a corrected copy of the handout after all the corrections are made.

Dialogue: A Sample Training Session in an Introductory Excel 97 Spreadsheet

Presented in dialogue 3.2 is an excerpt from a one-day introductory computer training class in an Excel spreadsheet. There were nine students (four males and five females) in the training class, and all were federal employees. Some of these employees were users of Lotus 1-2-3, also a spreadsheet by a different vendor, and they were transitioning to Excel. This part of the lesson lasted for approximately eight minutes. As part of the exercise, the students were expected to learn the maximum number of rows, columns, and cells that are allowed in the Excel 97 version.

The objective of the dialogue presented here is to explain the concepts of columns, rows, cells, and their naming conventions in a spreadsheet. After an introduction to the Excel inputting/editing screen and columns and rows and their name conventions, students engaged in a dialogue with the teacher.

To assist our readers in understanding this excerpt, we want to explain that the columns are labeled as A, B, C, D, and so on, whereas the rows are

Dialogue 3.1. Lesson on Using a Comma in English Nonfiction Writing

Note: Observations and/or comments of the teacher regarding a student or situation are italicized.[1]

Session Dialogue		Teaching Principles (*) Management Tactics (■) Illustrated
Teacher	Before beginning on the use of the comma, let's do a quick review of what a dependent and an independent clause are. Andrea, What is an independent clause?	* ■ * ■ Gain and maintain attention · Use Inductive approach · Call Students by name · Anchor new concepts to familiar experiences
Andrea	An independent clause is a sentence and can stand on its own. It has a subject, a verb, and a complement. For example, I came to our class today. In the example, I is the subject, came is the verb, and to our class today is the complement.	
Teacher	Right. What about a dependent clause, Bernadette?	
Bernadette	A dependent clause has the same things as an independent clause. But it has one additional thing, a signaler word.	
Teacher	Right on. What are some of those signalers, Celestin?	
Celestin	Since, because, if, when, although.	
Teacher	Good. Last week, we dealt with the use of the period and the question mark in writing. Chevelle, where do we use a period?	
Chevelle	At the end of a complete thought which is a sentence.	
Teacher	Exactly. What about a question mark, Elita?	
Elita	At the end of the question.	
Teacher	Good. Now, we need to move to the most misused and misplaced punctuation mark of them all. Does anyone have an idea?	
Kevin	Oh, yeah. The comma.	
Keyonna	I never know where or when to use it.	
Khadija	I sort of close my eyes and stick it in.	
Teacher	Welcome to the club. Most of us, myself included, have run into this problem. So today we will begin solving the problem of where to use a comma. On the screen (*a chalkboard or a flipchart could be used as well*) is a paragraph, with numbered sentences, from a student paper. Some of the	

(continues)

Dialogue 3.1. (Continued)

Session Dialogue	Teaching Principles (*) Management Tactics (■) Illustrated
commas are used correctly and some are missing. So let's begin with the first sentence. 1. When I was between the ages of 14 and 18, I ran the streets from morning to night and no one knew where I was. 2. Since I was taking care of myself I had come to the conclusion that I could come and go when I felt like it. 3. If something was happening I was there. 4. For example, a girlfriend's sister was having a party at this club and she invited me. 5. I knew that I was too young to go, but I couldn't let her know. 6. So I went and purchased a fake ID. 7. When Friday night came I was there drinking and dancing with the older men and no one ever found out that I was a minor.	* ■ * ■ Anchor new concepts to familiar experiences Call Students by name Use Inductive approach Gain and maintain attention
Teacher	Laverne, what do you see in the first sentence concerning a comma used, not used, or missing?
Laverne	There is a comma after the dependent clause, "when I was between the ages of 14 and 18." That's all there is.
Teacher	What makes it the dependent clause, Ofon?
Ofon	There is a signaler, when, at the beginning of the clause.
Teacher	Good. Do you think that the comma after the dependent clause should be there, Omar?
Omar	If I take it out, the sentence just goes on and on. Yes, I think it should be there. Moreover, there is a signaler, when, at the beginning of the sentence.
Teacher	That is very good. Now, look at sentence 2. Any similarities to sentence 1, Pamela?
Pamela	Yes, it starts with a dependent clause, and no comma comes at the end of it.

Teacher	So, what might we do?
Shonita	Put a comma at the end after the word "myself."
Teacher	Okay. Anybody see any other sentence like I and 2?
Todd	Yes, sentence 3.
Teacher	Good. What are you going to do?
Tracy	Put a comma after "happening."
Teacher	Right. Any other sentence?
Tsrha	Sentence 7. A comma could go after "came."
Teacher	You got it. After the comma, what kind of clause came next, Yasmin?
Yasmin	An independent clause.
Teacher	Exactly. It appears that the dependent clause was setting up for an independent clause. We can't have a sentence with a dependent clause only. Now, what conclusion might we begin to draw based on sentences 1, 2, 3, and 7?
Carol	All four started with a dependent clause. One had a comma at the end; the other three didn't. Now, all four do. So if I start a sentence with a dependent clause, I need to put a comma at the end to signal that I am now going on to the independent clause.
Teacher	Very neatly stated. We have found one use of the comma. Now, let's go back and look the sentences to see if we can find another. Billy, any thoughts on this? Look for coordinators. *(The session was continued.)*

Sidebar markers (vertical):
* Gain and maintain attention
* Use Inductive approach
■ Call Students by name
* Anchor new concepts to familiar experiences
■ Reinforcement

¹ English dialogue provided by Dr. Thomas S. Oliver, professor of English (retired).

named as 1, 2, 3, 4, and so forth. Also, in this session, dialogue is not limited to a teacher and students. In response to actions taken by the students at the teacher's instruction, the computer system itself now becomes a third participant in the session. The directions by the teacher in this session are directed to all of the students unless a particular student asks a question or makes a comment. Then, that student's name is used.

Well now, we have finally made it through this chapter dealing with the four basic teaching principles, and we have underscored that the easy and, unfortunately, time-honored teaching principle of deductive learning is not,

Dialogue 3.2.   A Sample Training Session in an Introductory Excel 97 Spreadsheet

Note: Observations and/or comments of the teacher regarding a student or situation are italicized.

Session Dialogue		Teaching Principles (*) Management Tactics (■) Illustrated
Teacher	What is the maximum number of rows in the spreadsheet? (*The new concept here is the maximum number of available rows in Excel for a single sheet. Students were already looking at their Excel screen and some of them are familiar with this arrangement of rows and columns.*)	* ■ * ■ Anchor new concepts to familiar experiences — Call Students by name — Use Inductive approach — Gain and maintain attention
Bill	22.	
Teacher	What do you think, Ed?	
Ed	200. (*Student has down scrolled the screen.*)	
Teacher	Do you agree, Robert?	
Robert	No. I have 5000. (*Robert was still scrolling down.*)	
Judy	Is there an easy way to find out this information?	
Teacher	We will try. **Press** the <End> key and then the <down-arrow> key on the keyboard.	
Computer	Displayed 65536 as the last row. (*Students were thrilled to discover that they have that many rows to work with if they wanted to.*)	
Judy	(*Smiled*) Now, I can tell you how many total columns there are in the spreadsheet.	
Teacher	Should we let her?	
Students	Why not?	
Judy	**Press** the <End> key and then the <right-arrow> key on the keyboard.	
Judy	The last column is labeled as IV	
Teacher	What does that represent in numerical terms? (*This is a difficult question, and the teacher really does not expect the right answer from students.*)	
Teacher	(*The teacher wrote, in short notations, the column names starting from A to Z, AA to AZ . . . and lastly from IA to IV. Anchoring new concept of labeling columns to student's experience of 26 letters in the alphabet.*)	
Karen	I think the answer should be 260.	
Teacher	Do you agree with this answer, Khim?	

Khim	No. The answer should be 256 because the column labeling does not go all the way to IZ, it stops at IV. Therefore, it is short of 260 by 4. (*Khim, an experienced user of personal computers was challenged with this question.*)
Teacher	That is the right answer, Khim. Well done.
Teacher	Press the <Ctrl + Home> key on the keyboard, and type = 256*65536 in cell A1.
Students	The answer is 16777216. (*Peter did not get the right answer, and could not even read the answer.*)
Teacher	Peter, can you tell us what the error message is?
Peter	My answer is 1.1E + 12 and I don't know what it means.
Teacher	Let me see. (*Looked at Peter's screen and discovered that he has typed = 256*65536*65536 in cell A1.*)
Teacher	Peter, you have just made a "good-error." Let me explain. (*Teacher saw an opportunity to explain scientific notation to the class. Explanations for the E notation are also contained in Excel Help.*)
Teacher	Can you read this number now, Peter?
Peter	Absolutely. The number is 1.1 trillion.
Teacher	Excellent, Peter.

* * Use of differential knowledge base
Capitalizing on student "good errors"

repeat not, one of them. As we said at the beginning of this chapter, four basic teaching principles lie at the heart of the successful teaching-learning process. They are: anchoring, inductive learning (versus deductive learning), accelerate slowly, and practice, practice, and practice = mastery. Within "accelerate slowly" are three guidelines: start where the learner really is; front-load the early part of the course with whatever key information the course depends on; and take time to explain, using analogies derived from the students' own experiences where appropriate. These teaching principles need to be adapted to your particular subject matter and your own style of management and then practiced to the point of full mastery so they are always at your fingertips.

But read on: there are some other advanced teaching principles to add to your repertoire, which, when mastered, will make your contact hours with students increasingly more productive.

NOTES

1. D. P. Kauchak and P. D. Eggen, *Learning and Teaching* (New York: Allyn and Bacon), 366, 2003.

2. Kauchak and Eggen, *Learning and Teaching*, 366.

4

ADVANCED PEDAGOGICAL PRINCIPLES

Now we come to what we call the advanced pedagogical principles. As you might expect, these principles are more complex and subtle, but they, like the basic ones, should be used every day. Naturally, they will take time, practice, and patience, as we have found out from our experience. Rome wasn't built in a day, and neither is great teaching. For each principle, we give a definition, provide a rationale for it, and present illustrations of it using different academic disciplines. In the examples that follow, you will be able to identify the use of the basic pedagogical principles and various management tactics as well. The principles presented here—when combined with those of the previous chapter and backed up by preplanning—are the *sine qua nons* of successful teaching.

"GOOD ERRORS"—NOT AN OXYMORON

What can we say that's good about an error when students make it in a classroom? Actually, quite a bit! First, the students are paying attention and are not intimidated, a crucial aspect for learning. Second, if nobody makes an overt error, as a teacher you may be completely unaware of the possible mistakes your students can and will make. Third, making an error can lead to improved understanding. In a subject such as computer applications (programming, in particular), people make mistakes all the time and are surprised at how much they learn from making them.

We look at the kinds of errors students make and typically refer to most of them as "good errors" because, if handled right, they can lead to clearer and more sophisticated understandings of the subject matter not only by the students but also by you as well. They enhance the quality of the interaction between students and you, the teacher. Some of the common types of good errors are partial answers to a question, an answer to something previously learned but tangential to the present discussion, and a response or comment that anticipates a future topic or content.

The real trick for the teacher is how to handle the good error. Landing on a student for the error is wrong. True, the student question or response is not correct, but it's a put-down. A teacher's response emphasizing the error is easy and all too often used. The right way is not so easy, but the payoff is well worth the effort. You must capitalize on the error and use it to further not only that particular student's learning but also the learning of all the other students. So what do you do? The right way involves continuously processing the nonverbal behaviors of the class as a function of your presentation, bearing in mind that you must always be observing as well as teaching. Also, you must be prepared to link in a positive way (and whenever possible in a humorous—and good-humored—way) a student's wrong or incomplete response, question, or comment to what the students are learning, what they might have learned, or what they may be learning in the future.

Let's provide some examples of good errors. Case 4.1 is taken from math.

CASE 4.1

In math, a common task is solving for an unknown quantity in a simple equation. This simple equation can be $0.5 X = 5$. The task is to solve for X. One of the students quickly raises his hand and says the answer is 0.1. I said, "You must have divided 0.5 by 5." Obviously a wrong answer to the question asked, but it is a "good error" and a common one. Instead of telling the student that the answer is wrong, I used it as an opportunity to emphasize the concept of the coefficient of an unknown quantity. I then asked, "What is the coefficient of X in this case?" Instantaneously, a couple of students responded with an answer of 0.5. I then asked, "What shall we do to solve for X?" Another student answers, "Divide the number on the right of the equal sign by the coefficient of X, which is 0.5." Another student responds, "The answer is 10." The student who gave the wrong answer the first time immediately recognizes what he has done. Now he says, "I did the division backwards," and he agrees with the other student's answer of 10.

What the students came to realize with my help was that everything must be divided by the coefficient of the unknown quantity to solve for the unknown. This concept is extremely important for students to learn, and as pointed out earlier, a common place for students to make mistakes.

Case 4.2 is from an introductory physics course.

CASE 4.2

I was teaching two new terms: speed and acceleration. In a physics course, the definition of terms and their units is very important. In this case, speed was already defined as distance divided by time. In the metric system, the students understood that the distance is measured in meters and time in seconds. The students also understood that the unit of speed is meters/sec in the metric system. All of this explanation is prologue to obtaining a definition of acceleration and its units from the students.

I then asked a student, "_____, please give us an example of acceleration." The student replied, "I would like to go from 0 to 60 [MPH] in three seconds in my car." Another student replied, "Acceleration could be change in speed in a specified time." This response is a layperson's definition of acceleration. Finally, a third student puts it all together. "Acceleration can be defined as change in speed divided by time." This is exactly the physics definition. I then asked, "What is the unit of acceleration in the metric system?" One student replied, "Meters per second?" This is a good error. I capitalized on this good error and told the student, "You mean the unit for the speed?" Student immediately agrees, "Yes, yes, yes!" No put-down occurred. The good error was connected to something the students had learned earlier and was used to reinforce the unit of speed. Eventually, another student, after a few minutes of discussion, came up with the answer "meters per second squared" as the unit for acceleration.

Case 4.3 is from a beginning social research course and is applicable both at the secondary and college levels across the social sciences and some of the humanities.

Good errors are very common in the classroom—particularly in the introductory course of any discipline. As a teacher, you will need to recognize them and then capitalize on them, instead of criticizing or ignoring a student for a wrong answer. Don't use contrasting language in handling a student's response, such as the word "but" or "however."

CASE 4.3

I often will ask the question, "What is the first task we have to do in carrying out a research study?" A student answers, "We will have to have some questions so we can ask people for their answers." This is a good error; it's a partial answer to the question and is one of the tasks of research, but it is not the first one. I answer, "You are right. It is one of the tasks. We do have to find some way of collecting information. Who else has an idea about what the first task is? " Another student responds, "We have to know what it is we're trying to find out?" I comment, "You are absolutely right. In research, we call it the 'statement of the problem.' And if we are doing survey research, the instrument with the questions comes a little later."

VIVA LA DIFFÉRENCE—CAPITALIZING ON STUDENTS' INDIVIDUAL DIFFERENCES

Students are different from one another, even when they all look alike. In today's public school classrooms, some students are ready to learn your subject matter, some may need a little more assistance—and reassurance—to do well, a few are stragglers who are able enough but have weak study and organizational skills, some are seriously unprepared—particularly in reading, and some don't give a damn. These are broad categories, but they provide a manageable way to view the variations in knowledge, skills, and values the students bring into your classroom. Your main task is somehow to reach and then teach them all—something positive. What does that mean? Hard work, of course, and figuring out what they do know and can do, including the last group mentioned. As a parenthetical aside, with regard to the "don't-give-a-damn" student or group, you must find out what lies behind this attitude, and you must do it individually. A quiet talk in private is often very revealing and can give you some insights into how to solve the problem or at least ameliorate it. This student cannot be ignored; you need to be a careful observer and, if necessary, seek help for the student.

Having said all this, how do you accomplish still another mission impossible? If they stay with you for the term, are able to participate, and are all still there at the end, then you have accomplished the task. Specifically, it means the swifties should not become bored in the class; the need-a-little-assistance students will have to be encouraged and helped; the stragglers assisted with studying and organizing their work; the unprepared strugglers will have to be worked with as best you can, and you will need to seek out resources available to them in the school and community. As with the difficult ones, a brief talk in private is helpful. Oftentimes, these students have chaotic or painful home lives and/or are seriously underprepared. Sometimes, a language problem is thrown into the mix as well. Find a way to help them so they stay and hopefully succeed in the class. Resources are sometimes found in some odd places like a church or a student club. And for some students, just being in a warm, well-organized, and comfortable place is enough, as the authors have found out over the years. While they may not pass the course, they may take something valuable away from it, which may simply include the experience with you, even though their experience is not reflected in a passing grade. And you may see them next semester coming back for another try. It's success of a different type for you as a teacher. You have shown these students that you do care.

As a teacher, you must continuously deal with three aspects that are associated with the often vast differences students bring with them into a classroom: ascertaining their knowledge base, assuring their full participation, and continuously assisting those who need help.

Ascertaining Students' Knowledge Base

At the beginning, you need to find out what the individual students of your class do know, and you must do it in a nonthreatening and nonjudgmental way. Keep in mind that a seeming dummy at the beginning of a course does not necessarily mean a dummy at the end of the term. The big rule is to avoid stereotyping. For example, a neat, well-dressed attractive student is often equated with being a bright student. To which we say, based on our experience, "Maybe yes, maybe no." On the other hand, a student who comes in looking sloppy and slouches around is all too often an immediate candidate for the "don't-give-a-damn" group. If you make these snap judgments, you will probably be in for some big surprises before you accurately sort the situation out. So here are several techniques for finding out if the students are ready to begin your course at the level you want them to be.

One technique, widely used by teachers, is pretesting on some critical aspects the students should have mastered before entering your course. Although this technique is easy for the teacher to use, in our opinion, it is really a complete "No, No." It can be labeled as "Intimidation 202." Even though you may assure them the results will not be graded and are strictly for your benefit, your students will be very suspicious and anxious about revealing what they don't know. For the seriously underprepared students, this technique can help to facilitate their early departure from your course because such a test can be overwhelming. For students who either feel or are shaky, the pretest can become a prologue to failure. So what might you do?

Instead of using a pretest technique, we note the most critical skills and knowledge students must have for the course on the agendas for the first few days of the courses to signal the importance of such skills and knowledge to the students and proceed to review them. This practice is a sophisticated application of front-loading. We don't just ask students about their familiarity and experiences with these skills and knowledge. Rather, we review them with students' participation to ascertain their differing levels of knowledge. Now, having said what we do in general, you now reasonably ask just exactly how it is done.

Cases 4.4 and 4.5 illustrate the process.

CASE 4.4

I proceed in the following way: on day one, I introduce myself and talk to these students about general course information for a few minutes. Then, I ask them to introduce themselves and also ask them to write their names on a sheet of paper so that I can refer to them later. In their introductions, I ask students, "When did you take the prerequisite, algebra, to this course?" "How do you feel right now about your knowledge and skills in that algebra course?" "Also, do you feel you might need some help?" Then I add, "It is perfectly OK to say, 'I do need help,' because I plan to review those aspects of algebra you will need for my course during the first week." With this assurance, the students open up, and I usually discover that a large number of them do need some "refresher" help in algebra.

In order to verify the accuracy of their assertions, however, I start reviewing the basic skills and knowledge for the items noted under review on the agenda. I ask students by name on a random basis from the list of their names to assist me in solving a problem when I am writing on the chalkboard. During the initial two-and-a-half-hour period, every student has been called on approximately eight to ten times. In the process, I learn a lot about their respective knowledge bases, where their deficiencies are, and, in short, who knows what. It also provides me with an idea of how much more review I will need to do.

Case 4.4 is a second course of introductory physics one of the authors has taught for a kazillion years, the most basic algebraic skills and knowledge needed for the course are working with the powers of 10, performing cross-multiplication, writing in scientific notations, and solving for an unknown in complex situations.

Taking time at the beginning to find out what they bring to the table is essential for later challenging the swifties and providing assistance to the stragglers. But it must be noted that the strugglers and the "don't-give-a-damns" don't usually appear in a course like this one.

Case 4.5 is an example from the other author who has taught Introduction to Social Science and Introduction to Sociology for the same kazillion years. However, in this course, stragglers, strugglers, and "don't-give-a-damn" types are definitely there.

CASE 4.5

Here is the technique I typically use. First off, I treat the students' life experiences as the prerequisite for the course. I introduce myself, describe my credentials, and provide general information about the course. Then, I pass out the syllabus and the agenda for day one. I next tell students, "Now, it's your turn. I have told you some things about me and this course, so you have some idea about what to expect. Now, I want to find out about you. Did you graduate from a D.C. school? If you didn't graduate here, where is your school located? Are you new to the U.S.? What is your major? Are you working?" For the occasional "don't-give-a-damn" and a probable swiftie (as smoke), I will often ask, "What made you decide to enroll in this course?"

Now bear in mind that I am not merely socializing or killing time. Here is where the role of being primarily an observer for a while becomes very critical. First, I learn a great deal about their communication skills and their confidence in their own learning abilities as they answer my questions. As they respond, their body language also tells me a great deal about their confidence and interest levels. Second, as each student provides basic information, I put together a preliminary assessment of a student's overall preparation, particularly with regard to the heavy reading and conceptual requirements of these courses. This assessment is very important since I will be forming students into preliminary work groups by the second day of the class. This assessment provides me with the "first take" on the differential knowledge base of each group of students. Third, this interchange subsequently will help me to tailor examples to what the students are probably interested in and know something about.

As they talk, I comment on the connection between their experiences and the forthcoming content of the course, making them feel they have a valuable contribution to make to the course. This commentary is particularly important to the international students (from Africa, the Middle East, Latin America, and Southeast Asia, to name some of the regions) who often have comprised about 50 percent of the class because most of the texts, particularly in sociology, deal almost entirely with the "American experience."

Ensuring Students' Full Participation

Having obtained all this information, what else do we do with it? We also use the information to make students feel they are contributing to the work of the class, a process that will continue throughout the entire term. Let us illustrate this process, using Case 4.6.

CASE 4.6

In a typical computer science course, a problem that appears on the horizon at the very beginning of a course is the way students compute an employee's gross pay. In this situation, I do not start by providing the equation to the students. Rather, the equation is to be derived from the students' inputs. I start with an employee who worked 50 hours during the week at the regular pay of $10.00 per hour, and overtime computed at time and a half of the regular pay rate. What follows uses the students' differential knowledge base. First, a student is asked by name. "————, what is the regular pay for this employee based on a 40-hour week?" ———— replies, "$400." I ask, "How did you arrive at an answer of $400?" The student replies, "I multiplied 40 by 10." I say, "Very good." Several students are then asked, "What is the overtime pay for this employee"? Eventually, one of them answers, "$150." I asked, "How did you get this answer?" The student responds, "I multiplied 10 by 10 times 1.5." Another student, totally puzzled, asks, "What do you mean? How did you get these numbers"? The student answers, "This employee worked 10 hours overtime. He was paid $10.00 per hour for the regular hours and time and a half for overtime." The student who asked the question nods, "OK." Now, I ask another student, "What is the gross pay for this employee for the week?" Several students now have the answer and respond, "$550."

Note: The students involved up to this point have average preparation. Now, the task for me is how to involve the more able students in a challenging way, but without losing the others.

What I do now is to equate the specific numbers of this example to general variables. I state, "HW is the variable for hours worked; ROP is the rate of pay; and GP is the gross pay." Several of the able ones are asked to provide a general equation for gross pay in terms of these variables for the employee who worked 40 or more hours. This is an important and not so easy question as these students found out, but they now possessed all the necessary information to set up the equation.

After about five to seven minutes of the interchange cited above between the students and me, the students suggested the equation as: GP = 40 * ROP + (HW − 40) * ROP * 1.5. Everybody is worn out by now, but the students are pleased with themselves. If appropriate, a short break can follow.

In addition to demonstrating the use of students' differential knowledge base, this example also illustrates several other pedagogical techniques: dividing a problem into finite steps, equal participation, and the inductive approach, going from the specific to the general case using the Socratic form of questioning.

Providing Timely and Ongoing Assistance

In order to ensure that every student succeeds to the maximum extent possible, we as teachers have the responsibility to monitor the progress of those who need help and then provide that assistance in a timely and ongoing basis. This may not always be possible, but we will provide two illustrations where it was done on an ongoing basis for every class meeting. Case 4.7 is the first example.

CASE 4.7

The course is Introduction to Physics II. The class usually meets from 5:30–8:00 p.m. twice a week. The emphasis of the course is on definition of terms and their units and on problem solving. What is being described here has been possible because of the block of time of almost 2½ hours. This practice may be difficult to implement if the class meets only for 45 to 50 minutes. Learning units of a physical quantity and problem solving are very important aspects in an introductory physics course. During my presentations, I will make sure that the unit of one of the physical quantities is not defined, for example, the refractive index. I will complete my presentation by 7:30 or so. I will then ask students to provide a unit for that physical quantity (refractive index) that I did not specify earlier, or I will ask the students to solve for an unknown quantity in the equation on hand. I will also tell them that once they provide the correct answer to it, they are free to go. This pronouncement sets an incentive in motion. Students are motivated to finish the problem as soon as possible. Those students who do not arrive at the answer will end up staying until the end of the class for further assistance. This technique allows me to focus more on these students in the next class meeting using similar concepts. The technique has worked like a charm because the students recognize they need to pay attention to the process of deriving units and problem solving. Also, the technique not only allows me to provide assistance when it is most needed but also enables me to offer it on an ongoing basis in the class. Of course, by now, I know who needs the most help.

Case 4.8, the second illustration, is taken from the social science area. The introductory course in social science is just loaded with unfamiliar concepts, theories, and terminology. The many definitions given are often italicized in the running context of each chapter of the text and then repeated at the end of that chapter, but the examples and illustrations are not. Sometimes there are only definitions and no examples in the chapter text itself. Many students simply become overwhelmed with the task of trying to keep all these terms and theories straight.

CASE 4.8

Wherever I can, I have used the inductive principle to elicit illustrations based on student knowledge, but sometimes I will assign the small work groups to emerge with what they think are appropriate examples, always making certain the less-prepared students do not cluster together. Then I check the illustrations the students develop and have them present the accurate and insightful examples with the terminology to the entire class. This practice allows the students to confer and assist one another, to experience success, and to avoid being isolated, alone, and inaccurate.

Often I will assign the three most critical terms in an area as homework and ask them for one additional example for each term after the term has been discussed and illustrated in class. By this time, they have several accurate examples, so the task is not in any way unfamiliar. I tell the students these examples can be taken from television, newspapers, personal experiences, books, or other resources.

A theory that has been discussed and illustrated in class will comprise a separate assignment, and only one application of it is required. I also let the students know they are free to consult with one another. Often I will use their examples in quizzes and other work in the class. Sometimes I incorporate their examples and explanations (giving due credit) into my notes for successive classes.

The important points to be gained from these examples are that the students have invested their own time and energy in the material, have made it their own, and will remember it for an extended period of time.

SETTING AND MAINTAINING HIGH EXPECTATIONS

It is easy to make the statement that teachers must set and maintain high expectations for all students. What we have discovered is if you don't know what actions to take to make this statement a reality, then it is simply a slogan and does not become translated into action. In order to communicate this message to students, first and foremost, you must firmly believe that no matter what a student looks like or what his or her social status is, that student can learn. If you don't believe this, then you are better off teaching elsewhere, rather than in a classroom filled with students with diverse backgrounds. You cannot hide your true beliefs regarding students' ethnic groups and learning abilities because through some mysterious osmotic process, the students will figure your beliefs out, and they usually do so with uncanny speed. Students are real people, and they are quite observant—it's crucial to their survival, particularly when they are minorities, new immigrants, and/or poor.

Over the years, we have put together some actions you can take that will consistently reinforce your belief in their ability to learn from you.

- Learn the students' names, and call them by name at every opportunity. Nobody wants to be called, "Hey, you." A name is a very important part of a person's identity, and students are impressed when you put out the effort to learn their names. You are telling them that they matter to you.

- Right from the start, make it clear there are no dumb questions. Their questions matter. Remember, it was Socrates who said, "The admission of ignorance is the beginning of wisdom." The big thing here is to establish that students are free to ask questions.

- In an earlier section, we mentioned the techniques for establishing the differential knowledge base. These techniques work very well in the maintenance of high expectations. Students' experiences, whatever they are, must be treated as valuable and relevant to your subject matter. This effort may take some really creative thinking on your part, but the payoff is well worth it.

- With new concepts or unfamiliar terms, don't assume the students will understand your pronunciation or accent. Write them on a chalkboard or a flipchart, and write big and clear. The students need to see them clearly and accurately. You understand you, but that doesn't mean they do. With any course having a lot of new terms, particularly true of introductory courses in any subject, the "hear, see, write" approach is critical because it will make use of three sensory pathways, a well-known reinforcement practice. And it doesn't hurt with the key terms to write their definitions as well.

- Like everything else in your course, good note taking is a learned behavior and requires practice. Check their notes, and if they are not adequate, then you need to teach them this skill, and as we have said before, teach them a three-level outline. Don't fall into the attitude of "The students should have learned the skills someplace else" or "It's not my job." It *is* your job because you are there to teach them. Your mantra should be "whatever it takes."

- We have observed that in simple arithmetic operations involving up to two-digit numbers, the calculator is a hindrance. The students lose confidence in their own ability to perform these operations, it creates an artificial dependency, and it slows them down. For example with operations like $6 - 13$ or 6^2, don't let the students use a calculator for them. If allowed to use the calculator for these kinds of operations, they often lose the skill of estimating what the answer should be. If the calculator gives the wrong answer based on what they have plugged in, they will believe that wrong answer. We have observed that requiring students to do these types of calculations mentally seems to be a real confidence builder, and a friendly competition on who gets there first with the right answer is set in motion. Also, as the course progresses, instead of you as the teacher verifying the right answer, let students do it among themselves.

- You must assign very limited and doable homework due at the next class period, and you should try to collect this homework in the next class meeting on an individual basis. Mostly in math, math-related, and science courses, the teachers will assign six to ten problems as homework, and that homework is usually to be turned in within a week. A few well-prepared students will try to complete as many problems as they can, but the less prepared quit doing homework because they are so frustrated with the difficulty level of some of these problems. When this latter group of students quits trying to do the homework, the stage is set for their failure. What we have discovered is if we assign a single task or a problem or two to be collected at the next class period, we usually achieve 100 percent participation. This approach with diverse student populations performs a miracle: a well-selected task is manageable and can be done in a reasonable time frame, which is important for these students since many of them have after-school jobs. Also, instruct them to consult with one another. A little peer teaching is a great confidence builder.

The use of these advanced teaching principles is further illustrated in dialogues 4.1 and 4.2, first one in computer science followed by one in physics. These principles are: good errors, capitalizing on students' individual differences, and setting and maintaining high expectations.

Dialogue: A Sample Lecture Session in Introductory Access Database Training Class

To be adequately understood, Dialogue 4.1 should be read *after* reading the explanation of Access Database. It is an excerpt from a two-day introductory computer training class in Access 97 database. To reiterate, the main objective in presenting this excerpt is to demonstrate some of the pedagogical techniques in action. This part of the lesson lasted for approximately forty minutes. As part of the exercise, the participants are expected to input a new record with their individual information for the fields in the table.

The subject matter objective of the excerpt presented here is to illustrate

Dialogue 4.1. A Sample Lecture Session in an Introductory Access Database Training Class

Note: Observations and/or comments of the teacher regarding a student or situation are italicized.

Session Dialogue		Teaching Principles (*) Management Tactics (■) Illustrated
Teacher	Everybody, insert a new record by **click-ing** on the New Record icon in the *Standard toolbar.*	
Computer action	Displays a blank 92nd record.	
Teacher	**Input** your last name in the ID field and try to type it in lowercase letters. (*The purpose here is to show that the system does not let students enter the information in lowercase letters. Also, they observe that the system does not take their full last name if it exceeds five characters and wouldn't let them leave the field if the last name contains less than five letters.*)	* ■ * ■ Anchor new concepts to familiar experiences Call students by name Use Inductive approach Gain and maintain attention
Students	We can't type in lowercase letters; the computer wouldn't let us. (*The application is designed to change all input for this field into uppercase letters.*)	
Teacher	That is OK for the time being because we will address this situation later on. Now, **press** the <Tab> key to move to the next fieldname.	
Gaby	I can't move. I have an error message. (*This is because Gaby's last name has fewer than five letters in his last name.*)	
Teacher	Exit the error message, Gaby. Now, **type** the first initial of your first name at the end of your last name and then **press** the <Tab> key. (*Gaby followed the instructions and moved to the next field along with other students.*)	
Teacher	**Press** the <down-arrow> key on the keyboard.	
Computer action	Error message: . . . required field . . .	
Teacher	**Exit** the message. Now **type** your office name in the Company Name field.	
Teacher	**Press** the <down-arrow> key.	
Teacher	**Close** the table. (*Students were dismayed that they might have lost the record they just entered. The teacher still did not comment, knowing that the record really was not lost.*)	

Teacher	**Open** the same table again and **move** to the end of this table where you have entered a record before.
Agnes	I told you we are going to lose this record.
Marsha	I have 92 records and not 91. I didn't lose my record. Where did my record go since it is not there?
Jeff	The new record is already in the alphabetical order.
Teacher	**Insert** a new record.
Computer action	Displays a 93rd record at the end of the table in response to Insert Record command.
Teacher	**Type** your last name one more time in the first field for Customer ID and **press** the <Tab> key to move to the next field.
Teacher	**Enter** information for Company Name and press the <down-arrow> key.
Computer action	Error message: . . . duplicate record . . .
Teacher	**Exit** the message window.
Teacher	**Delete** information from the CustomerID field.
Computer action	Error Message. (*The system will not let them.*)
Teacher	**Press** the <Esc> key twice. (*Everything was OK; the entire duplicate record was removed from the window.*)
Teacher	What did you observe during this data entry session, Valencia?
Valencia	I could not enter information in lowercase letters. (*Valencia was asked first to ensure a successful experience for her because she seemed to have the least exposure to computers and databases.*)
Teacher	What is your observation, Pat?
Pat	I could only type the first five letters of my last name in the Customer ID field.
Teacher	Can you add something to this, Gaby?
Gaby	I could not leave the Customer ID field without typing an extra character at the end of my last name.
Teacher	What about you, Agnes?
Agnes	I could not leave some fields empty in the table. (*The explanation usually follows during the creation of students' own table. This is just to show the capabilities of the system in various situations.*)

* Students' Differential Knowledge Base

(continues)

Dialogue 4.1. (Continued)

Session Dialogue		Teaching Principles (*) Management Tactics (■) Illustrated
Teacher	Can you tell us more about the data entry session, Marsha? (*The participants apparently with the most experience with computers and database and a very keen interest in them were asked questions last to challenge them.*)	
Marsha	The system automatically alphabetized the information for the first field name, Customer ID.	
Teacher	Did we leave anything out, Jeff? (*Jeff seemed to have the most experience and, therefore, was asked to respond at the end to provide a meaningful challenge.*)	
Jeff	I didn't have to save the data before I closed the table.	
Teacher	(*I provided summary of the interaction as follows.*) A database can be structured to limit data in a certain field in terms of its case or the number of characters; certain fields can be declared as required fields; Access tables can be closed without first saving the data and new data or changes to data are saved; certain fields can be automatically sorted by the database; and pressing the <Esc> key twice "undoes" what was done to a record, a lifesaving key in this program. (*I did not have to explain the reasons for the computer error/information messages because the answers became self-evident when students carried out the instruction I provided.*)	

techniques for controlling data entry in format and accuracy using the Input Mask formatting feature in the Access database. After an introduction to the Access database window, the students are expected to navigate an Access table provided in a file named *Northwind.mdb* that just happens to have ninety-one records in it. The typical fields in this table are Customer ID (identification), Company Name, Contact Name, and so on.

To assist our readers in understanding this excerpt, we want to explain that the structure of this particular table limits the customer ID field to five characters of a person's last name and this information can only be entered in uppercase letters. Also, if the last name of a student is fewer than five characters, the student needs to pad the last name with enough characters to make it five. Additionally, if the student's last name is more than five characters, the structure of the table under consideration will only allow that person to enter the first five characters. At the beginning of this lesson, however, the students do not have any idea about the structure of the table. They will discover it on their own after completing the teacher-directed exercise. One other point must be made: This session dialogue is not limited to a teacher–student interaction. In response to actions taken by the students at the teacher's instruction, the computer system now becomes a third major participant in the session. Also, the instructions in this session are directed to all of the students unless some student asks a question or makes a comment.

CASE 4.9

During this Access Database session, one student was closing his eyes often during the introduction phase. When I asked him to respond to a question, it was clear he was actually taking a nap. Obviously, he had worked an evening shift the day before. I had a choice: let that student continue taking a nap and, therefore, not learn anything, or I could intervene and wake him up so he could learn.

I had previously joked with this student several times and felt comfortable in intervening. I asked this student to provide instructions to the class for the next topic, already spelled out in the training book. The student really woke up and did not attempt to close his eyes again. This technique must be used carefully and cheerfully because a shy person might take it in a negative way.

Dialogue: A Sample Lecture Session in an Introductory College Physics II Class

To assist readers in the reading and understanding of this dialogue, basic information is provided first. Dialogue 4.2 is taken from a lesson plan in Introduction to College Physics II, discussed during the third week of class.

In the prerequisite course, Introduction to College Physics I, students learned about the physical quantities, their magnitudes, and units. Most students taking the course were familiar with an electrical circuit where at least three physical quantities are involved. These physical quantities are the voltage measured in volts, current measured in amperes, and resistance measured in ohms. Some students are also familiar with the fact that sometimes voltage is measured in millivolts (one-thousandth of a volt) and current in milliamps (amps is a short form of amperes).

The subject matter objective of this lesson was to study the dependence of current on voltage and resistance in a typical electrical circuit, amounting to deriving Ohm's law in an Introductory College Physics II class. A secondary subject matter objective was to anchor the concept of the magnitude of current, which might be quite new to students, from various sources that students are familiar with. The agenda shown in figure 4.1 was printed on colored paper for easy referencing and was distributed to all students. The topics here usually take two class sessions to complete, 2.5 hours each. Of the homework problems shown, three were solved in the class by the teacher. The remainder are similar problems to the three done in the class. Only one or two problems are actually assigned as homework per session.

Agenda for Chapter # 17 (Electric Potential)

Topics of Interest:
  1. Batteries
  2. Current
  3. Resistance and Ohm's law
  4. Resistances in series
  5. Resistances in parallel
  6. Resistivity and its temperature dependence
  7. Capacitors
  8. Capacitors in series
  9. Capacitors in parallel
 10. Energy stored in a capacitor

Homework Problems # 2,3,5,7,11,15,19

Figure 4.1.   A Typical Agenda in Introductory Physics II.

Dialogue 4.2 covers agenda items 1, 2, and 3. This interaction between the teacher and students took approximately seven minutes and most of the students experienced at least one instance of success. No student experienced a put-down. Each time a question was asked, enough time (three to five seconds or more) routinely was allowed for students to start responding.

There were nineteen students present on this day. The composite biography of the class was seven males and twelve females; two whites, four internationals, and thirteen African Americans. Their ages ranged from twenty-five to thirty-five years; all had the official prerequisites of algebra and College Physics I for the course. However, their academic preparation varied from underprepared to well prepared in terms of basic algebra, their mastering of that content, and in their general knowledge of the sciences. The class met from 5:30 to 8:20 p.m. in a typical physics laboratory.

The equations are:

$I \propto V$ and also
$I \propto 1/R$

Where $\propto$ is a proportional sign

I = current
V = voltage
R = resistance

combining these proportionalities into one equation leads to
I = (constant) V/R or $V = IR$ (which is Ohm's law).

❀   ❀   ❀   ❀

You have now completed the first section of the book, and all of the pedagogical techniques have been defined and illustrated in various ways. In the next section, you will meet the teaching principles and the management tactics again. The planning activities, the gateway pedagogy, are implicit in these chapters. Take your time to study, practice, and enjoy these chapters. After all, the computer programs can be fun, and we had a great time pruning the content to its essentials and applying at the pedagogical techniques.

Dialogue 4.2. A Sample Lecture Session in an Introductory College Physics II Class

Note: Statements that are teacher observations about a student or a situation are italicized and are enclosed in parentheses.

Session Dialogue		Teaching Principles (*) Management Tactics (■) Illustrated
Teacher	Khesha, what kind of batteries do you have in your home?	
Khesha	AA, AAA.	
Teacher	What are the typical voltages of these batteries, Eric?	
Eric	1.5, 3, and 9 volts.	
Teacher	What is the voltage, Ubong, of a car battery?	* ■ Gain and maintain attention · ■ Use Inductive approach · * Call students by name · ■ Anchor new concepts in magnitude of current and volt and Ohms law to students' experiences in voltage and current
Ubong	I don't know. (*An international student, bright, but shy and no experience with cars.*)	
Fitsum	12 volts. (*A student with lots of experience with cars.*)	
Teacher	How much current is typically supplied by the household's batteries, Scott?	
Scott	From milliamps to several amperes.	
Teacher	If a car battery is three to four years old and working perfectly during the summertime, but dies on the first cold day in winter, it cannot be supplying enough current to start the car. How much current is supplied by the car's battery at start-up when in good condition, Eric?	
Eric	10,000 amps. (*A student with familiarity in electronics.*)	
Teacher	Too high. What do you think, Cynthia?	
Cynthia	5,000 amps.	
Teacher	Still too high. Amie, what do you think the answer is?	* ■ Gain and maintain attention · ■ Use Inductive approach · * Call students by name · ■ Anchor new concepts
Amie	(*After a short pause, she responds.*) 750 amps.	
Teacher	Amie, you're getting close; a car battery can actually supply between 300 and 400 amps at start-up.	
Teacher	Do you know people who keep on cranking the car when it doesn't start, Maisha?	
Maisha	Sure.	
Teacher	What effect does the continuous cranking have on various parts under the hood, Maisha?	

Maisha	You flood the carburetor.
Bernadette	This drains the battery as well. (*An immediate follow-up comment.*)
Teacher	Right, Bernadette. What else could be happening, Gene, as a result of continuous cranking? (*Gene seems to know quite a bit about cars.*)
Gene	The wires near the battery post become very hot, and I have seen the insulation coming off the wires.
Teacher	Good . . . Now, Olushola, would you use a hair dryer that uses 120 volts in the United States in a country where the voltage is 240 V? (*An international student.*)
Olushola	No.
Teacher	Right. Can you, Solitare, explain the reason for it?
Solitare	The hair dryer will burn out because of too much current.
Teacher	Now, what type of relationship exists between current and voltage, Yasmin? (*A student well prepared for the course.*)
Yasmin	Current increases as voltage increases and . . . it seems there is direct relationship between them.
Teacher	That is very good, Yasmin. Now, keeping in mind that insulators have very high resistance and impede the flow of current, can you talk about the relationship, Julie, that exists between current and resistance based on what you have learned so far? (*Probably the best prepared student in the class.*)
Julie	Yes. Higher resistance means less current and I think that there is an inverse relationship.
Teacher	Excellent, Julie. Let us now summarize this discussion. (*What emerges as a function of this discussion is that students have varying degrees of familiarity with the concepts and applications of amperes and voltage terms. They also understand that higher voltage can burn something that uses current, with the conclusion being that higher voltage gives rise to higher currents and, in turn, produces lots of heat. The teacher then writes the following equations on the chalkboard with students nodding.*)

* * Use Differential knowledge base
* Challenge "Swifties"
■ Assure equal participation

5

HANDS-ON TRAINING IN PEDAGOGICAL TECHNIQUES USING UNIVERSAL COMPUTER APPLICATIONS

Chapters 5 through 11 comprise the second section of the book. Serving as the gateway chapter to the second section of the book, chapter 5 presents the perspective, purposes, and organization of chapters 6 through 11. In addition, it contains guidelines for a trainer or professor dealing with a group of students or for a staff development expert conducting a workshop or seminar in a school system as well as individual professionals pursuing the program on their own. Lastly, it provides instructions for loading the computer files necessary to the ensuing chapters of this section.

PERSPECTIVE

All of the chapters are written from the perspective of reinforcing the teaching principles and classroom management tactics presented and illustrated in chapters 1 though 4. We must clearly point out that the computer content is subordinate to the pedagogical techniques involved. This content is being used to reinforce and demonstrate these techniques, which to our knowledge has not been done in standard texts on pedagogy. The explanation undergirding our selection of computer subject matter for the pedagogical training is threefold: (1) trainees having expertise in a subject matter area, like math, will pay no attention to the pedagogical techniques demonstrated (Instead, they will focus on the content); (2) trying to teach pedagogical techniques in a vacuum will guarantee that they stay there; and (3) a new, less familiar, and useful content must be chosen in order to demonstrate the pedagogical techniques and their power. We reiterate that the computer subject matter included in this section does *not* constitute a manual for computer training.

PURPOSES AND ORGANIZATION OF CHAPTERS 6–11

Each chapter in this section, except for chapter 5, uses a variety of the pedagogical techniques described in chapters 1 through 4. As one would expect, some techniques are used more often than others, depending upon the difficulty of the subject matter topic and the diversity of the student population involved. Specifically, chapters 6 through 11 contain a brief overview of the subject matter topic and then apply selected pedagogical techniques to put across the particular topic to students. The examples included in the chapters are taken from actual classroom teaching sessions. Each example is labeled as a session dialogue.

In the presentations of session dialogues, the teaching principles and classroom management tactics that every professional reading this book needs to keep in mind are shown in the right column. The teaching principles are denoted by a star (*) whereas the classroom management tactics are represented by a box (■). Together, they comprise the pedagogical techniques or simply the pedagogy that has been used. Every professional must keep in mind that pedagogy, the art of teaching, permeates the computer content being used, even for those topics where no session dialogues are shown.

The session dialogues are actual excerpts of computer training sessions carried out by one of the authors. The dialogue between a teacher and a student or between a teacher and a group of students is shown in the first column and the pedagogical techniques are shown in the second one. Observations and/or typical comments of the teacher regarding either a student or a situation are italicized. In the computer session dialogues presented in the chapters for selected topics, a trainer or staff development expert assumes the role of a teacher. An individual reader who wants to become a teacher or who already is a teacher in another discipline assumes the role of a student in training. This role-playing should be followed throughout this section of the book whenever there is a dialogue shown. When teaching a group, the teacher should use actual names of the participating students.

For those topics where no dialogue sessions are provided, the trainer or staff development expert should convert these topics into session dialogues and continue to use appropriate pedagogical techniques (space considerations prohibited providing dialogues for every topic). Individual readers who are pursuing the program on their own should follow the instructions for completing each task, bearing in mind various pedagogical techniques are embedded in each task, such as sequencing.

The computer screen displays included in these chapters to illustrate various concepts are based on the Windows 2000 Operating System. These screen displays are comparable to those in Windows 95, Windows 98, and Windows NT. In other words, the procedures described here are just as appropriate for these other operating systems.

Throughout this section, the reader will encounter: (1) the computer screen displays (copies of what the user sees on a computer screen [Desktop] for a topic); (2) actual session dialogues between a teacher and students illustrating the pedagogy involved; and (3) tables that organize key information in column form for easy referencing.

In addition, certain formatting conventions are employed when a user is taking a certain action but not otherwise. They are:

- **Bolded** text signals an action to be taken by a user, e.g., **click**.
- <u>Underlined</u> text shows the name of the computer object, e.g., <u>My Computer</u>.
- *Italicized* text shows the location of the computer object, e.g., *Desktop*.
- Text that is <u>underlined and separated by a forward slash</u> (/) indicates more than one action, e.g., <u>View/Toolbars/Picture</u>. This means a user will first click on View in the menu bar and then on Toolbars and then Picture in the menus that follow.

In addition, for both the trainer and the individual reader, the session dialogues are to be completed before the exact answers or instructions for a task are read. The major purposes for following this sequence are to make the learner an active participant and, of course, to reinforce the new learning.

Authors' Note: This section is using computer applications as the subject matter content strictly to teach and reinforce pedagogical techniques. The computer content is subordinate to these techniques. Finally, we reiterate: these chapters are written strictly for those who (1) want to learn pedagogical techniques for themselves through the use of computer content, or (2) will be teaching others using this book as a text.

GUIDELINES FOR THE TRAINER, PROFESSOR, OR STAFF DEVELOPMENT EXPERT

When using this section of the book, these professionals should keep in mind they will need to assess the differential knowledge levels of participants in an unobtrusive manner before beginning any instruction.

Trainers in any setting must be prepared to vary examples if the participants demonstrate familiarity with the subject matter examples that have been used in the book. For example, if the participants are already familiar with the procedures of creating an outline and tables, then use creating an index or a table of contents as an alternative subject matter content to demonstrate the pedagogical techniques (See Case 5.1).

CASE 5.1

To cite a technique that has worked like a charm in computer training classes that one of the authors has taught, ask the participants to perform the following functions. First, I ask them to create a folder on the desktop. Second, I ask them to copy some computer files from a different folder on one of the drives available to them to the newly created folder on the desktop. Third, I ask them to start a computer application that is going to be taught. These three actions always provide me with a substantial amount of information about participants' knowledge of a personal computer and their ability to use it effectively.

Also, when using this book, I vary the content in the examples cited in this section of the book if the participants are already familiar with the subject matter content that is included. Other professionals or trainers should do likewise.

GUIDELINES FOR THE INDIVIDUAL READER

For individual professionals reading this book on their own who want to learn the pedagogical techniques illustrated through the examples included in this section, they, too, will need to assess their own knowledge of the subject matter content used to illustrate the pedagogy. If the content of a particular topic is new, then this content must be read and practiced. If a subject matter topic is not new, then only its presentation in the dialogue sessions must be read and practiced to see the pedagogical techniques in action.

INSTRUCTIONS FOR LOADING COMPUTER FILES ONTO YOUR COMPUTER

Before working with the remaining section of this book, you will need certain computer files and templates provided on a CD accompanying this book. The computer files for chapter 6 are chosen to familiarize users with the names, size, type, and date characteristics of computer files. The files for chapters 7 and 8 are templates to be used with those chapters. The instructions for loading these files on to your computer in appropriate directories are, as follows:

1. **Insert** CD in CD-ROM Drive (typically drive D:). A window should pop up with a listing of menus. Just follow instructions on the CD. If you do not see a window, then continue with the following instructions for loading the necessary files.
2. **Click** Start on the left side of the *Taskbar*.
3. **Click** Browse.
4. **Locate** the CD-ROM Drive icon from the *<Drop-down>* list of objects, and then just follow instructions on the CD. The system will create the necessary directories and copy all the required files.

Once you have completed these steps, you are ready to begin the rest of the chapters comprising this section and the hands-on experience provided in them. We think you will find the chapters that follow both challenging and informative. You are off on your pedagogical adventure.

6

THE BASICS OF THE PERSONAL COMPUTER

This chapter presents the basics of the personal computer intertwined in a systematic way with pedagogy. The translation of this mouthful is that there is no escape from pedagogical techniques—they permeate every topic we are teaching you.

Smile: It'll get better.

Each topic on a personal computer is carefully sequenced, and pedagogical aspects are identified for those topics where the session dialogues are sufficiently compact and self-contained. These dialogues show the reader more clearly that pedagogy is inherent in the teaching of every topic.

Currently, almost all IBM and IBM-compatible personal computers use the Windows Operating System. One big advantage of Windows is that it eliminated the need for memorizing a series of commands. Another is that Windows also provides a friendly graphical user interface (GUI, pronounced "gooey") for assisting users in their daily work on a personal computer. Windows Operating System displays a Desktop with icons and a Taskbar. A typical Windows computer screen display (CSD) is shown in figure 6.1.

The Windows Desktop either contains icons, like the My Computer icon, or the space is blank like the writing surface of a desk. The Taskbar, usually located at the bottom of the screen, has the important Start button to its left and the time display on the right. In between these two icons, the Taskbar can contain either the application icons (the minimized window for a computer software program, like Adobe Photoshop, Word, or Excel) or shortcuts for other computer applications for ease of use. In addition, many

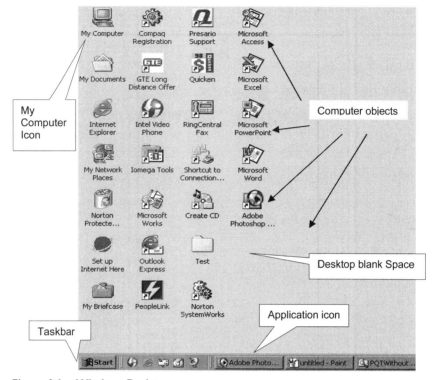

Figure 6.1. Windows Desktop

different types of computer objects are identified, such as program icons on the Desktop, icons on the Taskbar, the Taskbar itself, the empty Desktop, and so forth.

Now, with all of that said about the Windows Operating System, your next task is to learn how to use the mouse in an efficient manner in order to manipulate Windows with ease. This leads us to various techniques that are useful in dealing with Windows and the key actions that you can take with the mouse, your gateway to the personal computer.

GATEWAY TO THE COMPUTER: THE MOUSE

You can input information to the computer through a keyboard, joystick, screen, scanners, credit card readers, computer mouse, and so on. In Windows, the mouse is the dominant gateway to a computer. Without knowing its capability, you as a user restrict your use of a personal computer to a large extent. This is an example of ignorance *not* being bliss.

There are five basic mouse actions; they are first illustrated in dialogue 6.1. Observations and/or typical comments of the teacher in a dialogue session regarding a student or situation are italicized and are enclosed in parentheses. When teaching a class, you, the teacher, should use the actual names of the participating students.

Dialogue 6.1. A Sample Dialogue Session for Mouse Actions

Session Dialogue		Teaching Principles (*) Management Tactics (■) Illustrated
Teacher	We're going to learn the mouse actions first, followed by practice with these mouse actions. Before we do it, let me ask you a few questions. Anyone in the class who has not used the mouse before? (*Most people have some familiarity with the mouse.*)	■ * ■ ■ Gain and maintain students' attention * Use inductive approach ■ Call students by name
Teacher	What actions can we take with the help of the mouse, Jackie?	
Jackie	I can click on computer stuff.	
Teacher	OK. That is an action. Lorrie, what else can you do?	
Lorrie	I can double-click on items to open them.	
Teacher	Another action. Can the mouse help you do something else, Bill?	
Bill	It can help me to drag things, I have heard, but I don't know how to do it.	
Teacher	We will very soon learn how to drag objects with the mouse. Steve, do you have something else to add to this discussion?	
Steve	Oh yes, I can right-click with the mouse, but I never knew why I am doing it.	
Teacher	We'll get to the explanation of it soon.	
Teacher	Al, read the explanations of mouse actions as printed in Table 6.1. (*Individual students read each of the explanations. It is done to engage students in their learning. After this process was completed, the teacher then emphasized the difference between click and double-click.*)	

PRACTICE WITH THE MOUSE ACTIONS

1. **Point** the mouse to the <u>Time Location (clock)</u> in the *Taskbar*. It shows the day, month, and year as shown in figure 6.2.
2. **Click** on the icon for <u>My Computer</u> on the *Desktop* to select the object.
3. **Right-click** on the <u>Desktop</u>. You will see a list of actions in the form of a menu, called a pop-up menu. Now, **Right-click** on any of the program icons (like MSWord), and you will see another pop-up menu of the actions that you can take for the icon. The pop-up menus are shown in figure 6.3.

    In a similar way, you can <right-click> on other objects, like the Taskbar, and browse through the properties of these objects. You notice the actions you can take for a particular object are different and predetermined. You cannot make up the music as you go along.
4. **Double-click** on the icon for <u>My Computer</u> to open the window. The My Computer window opens up.

MANIPULATE A WINDOW

You can manipulate windows in at least six different ways: minimize, maximize, restore, close, resize, and move.

Open a Window

Double-click the icon for <u>My Computer</u>. This opens a window for My Computer. The icons for physical drives[1] (Floppy Drive, A:; Hard Drive, C:; Zip Drive, D:; and CD-ROM, F:) and Control Panel are displayed in figure 6.4. You can change the way the icons are displayed by using the View command in the Menu bar, and then you can select any one of the choices of large icons, small icons, list, or details to display the same infor-

---

1. If your PC is connected to a server, logical drives (F:, H:, S:, etc.) will also be displayed in the "My Computer" window. Don't worry about them. They are used when programs or files are to be shared with other users.

Table 6.1.   Explanation of Mouse Actions

Action	Procedure
Point	Position the mouse pointer on an item.
Click	Position the mouse pointer on an item, press the left mouse button, and then release the mouse button to select or highlight an object. *A Click always means Left-click.*
Double-click	Position the mouse pointer on an item, press the left mouse button twice in rapid succession to execute a program or open a folder. *A Double-click always means left Double-click.*
Click & Drag	Position the mouse pointer on an item. Press and hold the left mouse button and then move the mouse. When you are finished dragging this item, release the mouse button. This action results in moving that item, e.g., a window, from one location to another.
Right-click (inspector)	Position the mouse pointer on an item, press the right mouse button, and then release the mouse button. This allows you to look at the properties of a selected object, such as Desktop, Taskbar, and an icon.

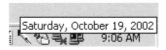

Figure 6.2.   Screen Display When a User Points to the Time Location

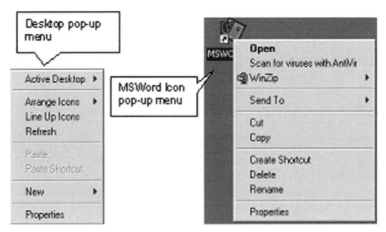

Figure 6.3.   Pop-up Menus for a (1) Desktop and (2) MSWord icon

mation in different ways. You can decide for yourself what the best arrangement is for you.

Minimize a Window

Click on the Minimize button (_) on the top right corner of the My Computer window. This will minimize the window, and the icon for it will be displayed on the Taskbar as an application icon as shown in figure 6.5.

Maximize and Restore a Window

1. **Click** on the application icon for My Computer on the *Taskbar* to open it again. This will bring the My Computer window on the Desktop to the size it had before it was minimized.
2. **Click** on the Maximize button (□) on the top right corner of the *My Computer* window. This will maximize the window (full screen), and the button for Maximize will change to a button for Restore, two over-

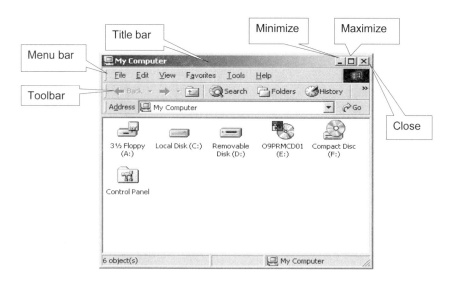

Figure 6.4.   My Computer Window with Its Various Parts

Figure 6.5.   Desktop Taskbar with Application Icons

lapping squares (⊟). Usually, it is not easy to resize a window when it is maximized.

3. **Click** on the <u>Restore button</u> (⊟) located between minimize and the close buttons on the top right corner of the *My Computer* window. This will restore the window (partial screen) to its original size, and the button you have just pressed will change back to the Maximize button.

Resize a Window

Point the <u>mouse</u> to one of the *borders* of the window. When the pointer turns into a two-headed arrow, **click** and **drag** the mouse to the new size of the window. This way you can change the size of the window from one side only. In order to resize the entire window from both sides, **point** the <u>mouse</u> to one of the *corners of the window*, wait for the pointer to change to a two-sided arrow, and then **click** and **drag**. Resizing allows you to display more than one window at a time. This is helpful when you are using multiple programs simultaneously, like Word, Internet, and e-mail.

Move a Window

Point the <u>mouse</u> to the *title bar* of the window, figure 6.6. **Click** and **drag** the window to a new location.

Close a Window

Click on the <u>Close button</u> (**✗**) on the top right corner of the window. When you open the window again, only a partial window will be displayed that can be maximized or resized.

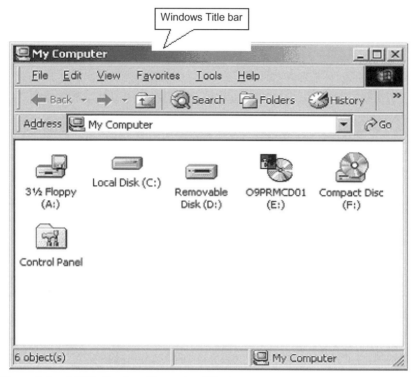

Figure 6.6.   A Title Bar in a Computer Window

THE IMPORTANT "MY COMPUTER" ICON

The My Computer icon allows you to see what hardware is installed on your computer in terms of floppy and hard drives, CD-ROM, a Zip Drive, or other peripherals.

1. **Double-click** on the My Computer icon on the *Desktop*. The My Computer window in figure 6.7 shows that there is a floppy drive (A:), hard drive (C:), a zip drive (D:), and CD-ROM drives (E:) and (F:). These objects are not underlined because they are just being identified. No user action is required. In addition, there is a folder for Control Panel that contains many other icons.
2. **Right-click** the Local Disk (C:) icon in *My Computer* window. The pop-up menu shown in figure 6.8 appears.

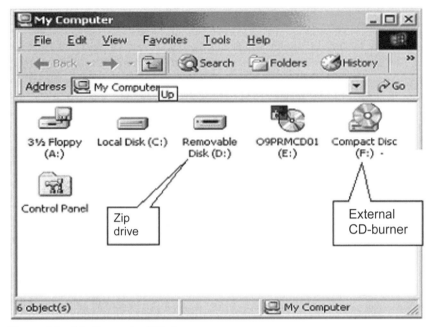

Figure 6.7. My Computer Window

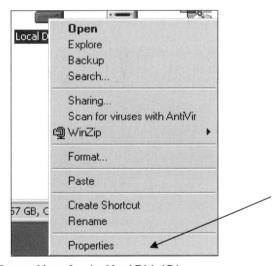

Figure 6.8. Pop-up Menu for the Hard Disk (C:)

3. **Click** on the Properties choice in the *pop-up menu*. The properties of the hard drive (shown in figure 6.9) are displayed. It shows that the capacity of this drive is about 10 GB (GB means a giga[billion] bytes). A byte is a character or a keystroke on a computer keyboard. So, gigabytes means a billion bytes, which is a humongous space—at least for the time being. As shown below, half of this capacity is space already used by computer files and folders. The other half is free space that is all yours, so you won't have to live 182 years in order to fill up the rest of the space.

4. **Right-click** the 3½ Floppy (A:) icon in *My Computer* window, and then **Click** Properties in the *pop-up menu* for the A: drive. Figure 6.10 is displayed in response.

5. **Double-click** on the Control Panel folder in the *My Computer* window to see the contents of this folder. The contents of the control panel are displayed in figure 6.11. Each icon allows you to take various

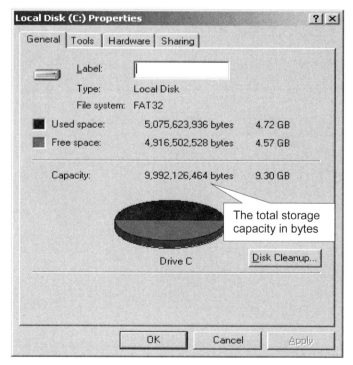

Figure 6.9. Properties of the Hard Drive (C:)

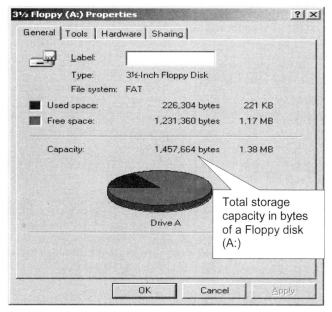

Figure 6.10. Properties of the Floppy Drive (A:)

actions for that object (icon). The mouse icon allows you to customize various properties of the mouse. For example, if you are left-handed, you can use this particular icon to change the mouse setting for yourself, since it is set for a right-handed person. This is a rare instance of your personality having some control over the computer.

MANAGE WORK ON THE COMPUTER

Now that you have learned how to use a mouse and manipulate Windows, you need to know how information is organized on a computer so you can store your own work in an organized way.

Information Organization in Folders and Files

1. **Double-click** the My Computer icon on the *Desktop.*
2. **Double-click** Hard Drive C:/Program Files/Microsoft Office/Office/

Figure 6.11. Contents of the Control Panel Folder

<u>Samples</u> to open the samples folder. The specific steps are: **double-click** on the C: drive, followed by **double-clicking** on the folders for <u>Program files</u>, <u>Microsoft Office</u>, <u>Office</u>, and <u>Samples</u>. Finally, you will arrive at the contents of the Samples folder shown in figure 6.12. Please note the location of the column headings for filename (or simply Name), filesize (Size), filetype (Type), and the creation or the change date of a file (Modified).

Get ready now for an actual walk-through in the uses of the column headings (dialogue 6.2).

Techniques for Selecting Files

You can either select individual or multiple files. To select a single file, click on the icon for that file. Multiple files can be selected in two different ways; they can be either contiguous or noncontiguous. This capability will save you time when you are copying, moving, or deleting many files at the same time.

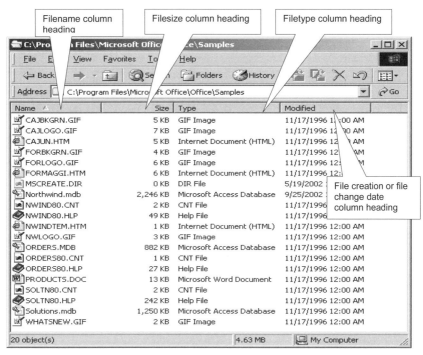

Figure 6.12.   Detailed View of the Contents of a Folder Labeled Samples

1. **Click** the first, second, and fifth files. With this command, you will select one file at a time.
2. **Click** on the first file again. Now **hold** the <Shift> key down and keep it down and then **click** on the fifth file. This action will select five contiguous files.
3. **Click** on the first file again. Now **press** the <Ctrl> key and keep it pressed. Then **click** on the first, third, and sixth files. This action will select three noncontiguous files. This kind of selection is displayed in figure 6.13.
4. **Press** <Ctrl-A> to select all files in the window. Maybe, you want to change your mind? Ok. It's called deselecting.

Authors' Note: You must practice these steps a whole lot to minimize teeth gnashing later on.

Dialogue 6.2.   A Sample Dialogue Session for Sorting Information in a Folder

Below is an excerpt from an actual computer training session

Session Dialogue		Teaching Principles (*) Management Tactics (■) Illustrated
Teacher	How many types of information are displayed in this window, Julie?	* ■ * ■
Julie	Four types. (*Someone might have five; the fifth one for file attributes.*)	
Teacher	What are those types, Karen?	
Karen	Name, size, type, and modified.	
Teacher	You mean filenames, filesize, etc.	
Stu	I think so.	
Teacher	**Click** on the <u>Name</u> column heading. Did you see any change in the display of information, Troy?	
Troy	Not yet. (*Because the information stays in the ascending order.*)	
Teacher	**Click** on the <u>Name</u> column heading again. Did you see any change now in the display of information?	
Students	Yes. A filename starting with the W is first.	
Cathy	Oh, yes, yes, yes. I see the filenames are arranged in the reverse order.	
Teacher	Yes, that's right, it is displayed in reverse alphabetical order, but in computers we call it descending order.	
David	Yes, I should have known that. (*Students have heard this term before.*)	
Teacher	**Click** on the <u>Size</u> column heading. Did you notice any change, Susan?	
Susan	Zero is first and a high number is last.	
Teacher	You mean the Size column is sorted in the ascending order?	
Maya	That is exactly what I meant.	
Teacher	**Click** in the <u>Size</u> column header again. What change do you see now, Satish?	
Satish	The column is sorted in the descending order.	
Teacher	What is this KB business after the numbers, Ibrahim?	
Ibrahim	I have no idea.	
Teacher	Are you sure?	

The right-hand column lists vertically:

Gain and maintain attention
Use inductive approach
Call students by name
Anchor new concepts of sorting information in computers to everyday experiences of sorting.

Martha	Maybe, I do. I am not sure and I am going to guess. This might stand for a kilobyte. Is that right?
Teacher	Absolutely. **Click** in the Size column header again. Now, look at the last number in the Size column. The number is displayed as 2,246 KB. Can you write this number in some other way?
Kevin	The number is two thousand two hundred forty six kilobytes.
Teacher	I agree. But can you write this number in terms of megabytes, Alex?
Alex	. . . I believe so. The number can be written as 2.246 MB.
Teacher	That is excellent. Now, **click** in the Type column header. Is the information organized in an ascending or descending order, John?
John	In an ascending order.
Teacher	Can you provide some examples of file-types?
Students	DOC for a word document, WPD for a WordPerfect document, MDB for an Access database, GIF for a graphics file.
Teacher	This is great.

* Use differential Knowledge base
■ Challenge "Swifties"
* Assure equal participation
* Provide clarification and emphasis for students' answers

ELECTRONIC ORGANIZATION IN FOLDERS AND FILES

In computers, information is stored in files, for example, a Word file, a PowerPoint file. Eventually, the number of files you have will increase to a large number. When that happens, you will need to organize your files into folders/directories and subdirectories. A folder may contain other folders and files, or it may just contain files. When we organize information in files and folders, we term it electronic organization of information. A computer organizes all of its programs and applications in this way so as to function efficiently and to carry out the tasks assigned to it by you in the fastest way possible.

Display of Folders, Subfolders, and Files

Windows Explorer is a program within the Windows Operating System. When opened, it will display information about Windows, folders, and files. Got that, everybody? Stay tuned; we'll try to explain.

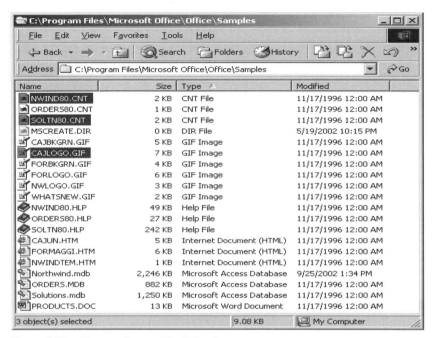

Figure 6.13. Noncontiguous File Selection

1. **Right-click** the <u>Start</u> button on the *Taskbar* and then **click** on
   <u>Explore</u>. One such display is shown in figure 6.14. The display by
   Windows Explorer is divided into two panels. The left panel is called
   the Folders window and contains all the folder names. The right panel
   is called the Contents window and displays the contents of the particular folder that is either open or highlighted. To repeat, the contents
   of a typical folder can be either files or folders or both (right panel).

      Now let us examine the Folders window in more detail. We point
   out that a plus (+) sign to the left of the folder or drive indicates that
   the directory is collapsed (all of its contents are *not* shown in the Folders window). In contrast, a minus (−) sign to the left of a folder rep-
   resents a folder that is expanded (all of its contents are shown in the
   Contents window). You might have to click on the minus (−) sign to
   the left of the C: drive to obtain the display shown in figure 6.15.

      A typical display of folders with expanded directories is shown in
   figure 6.15 for the C: drive. **Click** on the plus (+) sign to the left of

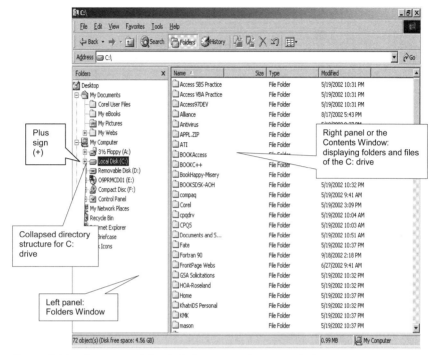

Figure 6.14. Contents of the C: Drive under Collapsed (+) Directory Structure

the *C: drive* if the minus sign is not already there. The C: drive now has a minus (−) sign to its left in the expanded mode for directory structure.

2. **Double-click** the folder for <u>Program Files</u> in the *left panel* to open the folders and expand the directories. You may have to scroll down (vertical scroll bar as shown in figure 6.15) in the Folders window to locate the folder labeled Program Files. The right-hand panel, the Contents window, will display all of the contents of the folder, including other folders and files. You may have to scroll down in the Contents window to view the files as well. If the window is not filled, no scroll bar will appear.

3. **Double-click** the folder for <u>Microsoft Office</u> in the *left panel* (figure 6.16), the Folders window, to open the folder and expand the direc-

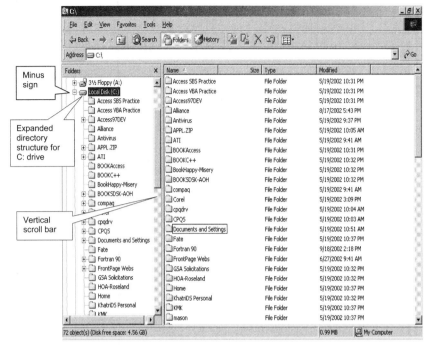

Figure 6.15. Contents of the C: Drive under Expanded (−) Directory Structure

tory structure. The Contents window will display all the contents (folders and files) of the folder labeled Office.

4. **Double-click** the folder for Office in the *left panel* (figure 6.16) to open the folder and expand the directory structure. The Contents window will display all the contents of the folder labeled Office.

5. **Double-click** the folder for Samples (highlighted) in the *left panel*. The Contents window will display all the contents of the folder, in this case all the files of the Samples folder. An illustrated display is shown in figure 6.16 with Samples as a subfolder for the Office folder. In turn, Office folder is displayed as a subfolder for the folder labeled, Microsoft Office.

Create Subject Matter Folders (Directories)

For this section, let us do a little role-playing. Assume you are the high school teacher who taught algebra and geometry to ninth graders during

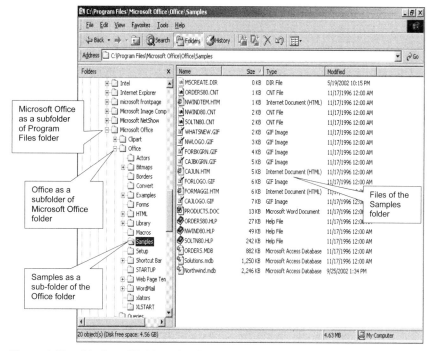

Figure 6.16. Display of Folders, Subfolders, and Subfolder Contents

academic year (AY) 2001 and pre-algebra, algebra, and pre-calculus to twelfth graders during AY 2002. You want to organize class work for these courses in computer folders. Your folder organization on the computer might look like the one shown in figure 6.17, with all the subfolders in place:

- Math is a folder of the C: Hard drive;
- AY 2001 and AY 2002 are subfolders of the Math folder; and
- Algebra and Geometry are subfolders of the AY 2001 folder, and so on.

Now let's see how to do this task.

1. Create the Math folder
   1.1. **Click** on the <u>minus sign</u> (−) to the *left of the C: drive* to collapse directories.

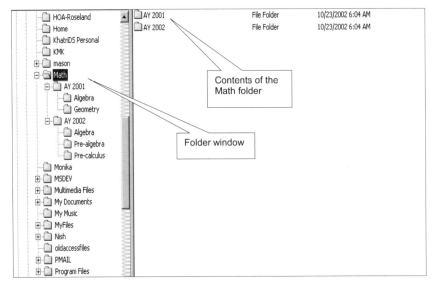

Figure 6.17. Partial Display of Folders and Subfolders for Your Courses

1.2. **Click** the C: drive (the letter C) on the *left-hand panel*, the *Folders* window.

1.3. **Click** on File/New/Folder (figure 6.18) either in the *Menu* bar or the *submenus*. These actions will display a folder in the Contents window under a name, New Folder. This is one way of creating new folders. (Some other ways will be used later on during the training.)

1.4. **Type** Math for the New Folder name in the *Contents* window and **press** the <Enter> key. As a precaution, when the folder

Figure 6.18. Creating a New Folder under the C: Drive Using the Menu Bar

labeled New Folder appears in blue, do not click on the folder. Just type the new name, Math, over the New Folder text in blue. Options you have if you create a mess (which can often happen):

- If you click on the New Folder icon inadvertently, delete the text for the folder, type its new name, and press the <Enter> key.
- If you happen to press the <Enter> key by mistake when the folder name appears for the first time in blue, you can change the folder name by using <right-click> on the folder, and then by selecting the Rename choice from the pop-up menu.
- If everything else fails, delete the folder and start over.

2. Create the AY 2001 subfolder

   2.1. **If you cannot see your folder for Math immediately, scroll down** and then **click** on it to open this folder.

   2.2. **Right-click** in the empty space of the Contents window.

   2.3. **Click** New and then Folder in the *pop-up menus* (figure 6.19). The system will create a folder, New Folder.

   2.4. **Type** AY 2001 for the name of the subfolder and then **press** the <Enter> key.

3. Create the AY 2002 folder and subfolders.

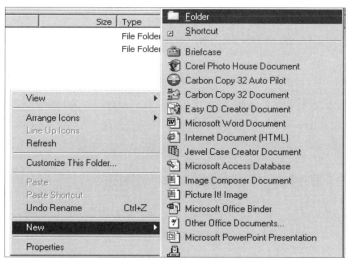

Figure 6.19. Creating a New Subfolder under the Math Folder Using <**Right-Click**>

Dialogue 6.3.   A Sample Dialogue Session for Creating Subject Matter Folders and Subfolders

Below is an excerpt from an actual computer training session

Session Dialogue		Teaching Principles (*) Management Tactics (■) Illustrated
Teacher	How do we create a new folder for AY 2002, Billie?	* ■ * ■
Billie	**Click** on the Math folder. **Right-click** in the blank space on the *right hand panel.* **Click** on New and then on Folder. Last step is to **type** AY 2002 for the name and **press** the <Enter> key.	*Practice with learned concepts* *Call students by name* *Use inductive approach* *Gain and maintain attention*
Teacher	How do you create a new folder for Algebra under the AY 2001 folder, John?	
John	**Right-click** in the blank space of the *Contents window.*	
Teacher	Are you sure?	
William	No. But I think I got it now. First **click** on the AY 2001 folder. Then you **right-click** on the *Contents window.* Next, you **click** on New and then on Folder in the *pop-up menus.* Finally, **type** the name of the folder as Algebra.	
Teacher	Terrific. Now, how do we create a new folder for Geometry under the AY 2001 folder, Steve?	
Steve	Same as before.	
Teacher	True enough. But I want you to walk everyone in the class through these steps again.	
Students	OK. Let me start. First, **click** on the AY 2001 folder. Then you **right-click** in the *Contents window.* Next, you **click** on New and then on Folder in the *pop-up menus.* Finally, **type** the name of the folder as Geometry.	
Teacher	How are we doing so far?	
Students	Great.	
Teacher	Now, let us try to create subfolders for the AY 2002 folder. Let us ask Dorris to walk us through the steps for creating a subfolder Pre-algebra for the AY 2002 folder.	

Dorris	First **click** on the AY 2002 folder to make it current. Then you **right-click** in the *Contents window*. Next, you **click** on New and then on Folder in the *pop-up menus*. Finally, **type** the name of the folder as Pre-algebra.
	(Two other students helped to create the remainder of the two folders for Algebra and Pre-calculus by following the steps mentioned earlier.)

SELECT AND COPY FILES

Selecting and copying files from one location to another is a common, everyday task. Oddly enough, many users make a mess, losing files or putting them in the wrong places, and thereby enduring much pain. To this pain and the "blue" language that goes with it, we underscore there is no "quick and dirty" way to learn this task. Here is how you do it.

Before you start the copying process, you must first identify both the source and destination locations for the particular file involved. The source location is where the file is. The destination location is where the file will wind up after being copied. In this process, you do not remove a file from the source location; the file stays intact in the original location. You can copy more than one file in this process. This is just like duplicating.

A folder labeled Chapter6 has already been created as part of chapter 5. This folder contains files of various types and sizes (figure 6.20). You are going to copy files from this folder to other locations.

Selecting and copying can take place in three different ways, which are shown below. Let's practice this technique.

1. Copy a single file
   1.1. **Click** the source folder, Chapter6, on the C: drive in the *Folders window* to open it. This folder is a hodgepodge of stuff, and its contents need to be organized into some order. For example, tests in the algebra course sitting in the folder labeled Chapter6 need to be filed into a subfolder labeled Algebra under the AY 2001 folder.
   1.2. **Click** in the column heading for Filename to sort files in ascending (alphabetical) order.

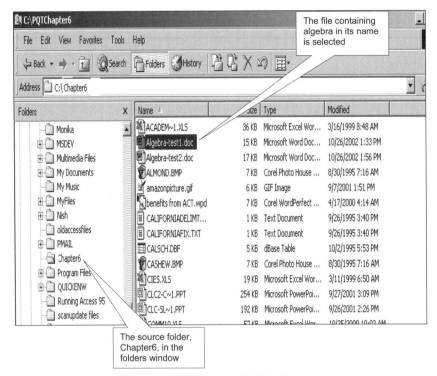

Figure 6.20. Partial Display of the Chapter6 Folder Contents

1.3. **Click** on the file that has <u>algebra</u> in its name. Click selects a file.

1.4. **Right-click** in the selected filename and then **click** <u>copy</u> in the *pop-up menu* (figure 6.21). These actions will place the selected file in the *clipboard*, a portion of the computer memory.

As a warning, don't click outside the selection because that will deselect the file, and then you must select it again before you continue with the copying process.

1.5. **Click** the <u>Algebra</u> subfolder in the *Folders window* under folder *AY 2001* to open the Algebra subfolder.

1.6. **Right-click** in the <u>Contents window</u> (the blank space on the right-hand side) of the folder and then **click** <u>paste</u> in the *pop-up menu* (figure 6.22). Figure 6.22 shows two actions, the <right-click> and Paste. These actions will copy the file from the clipboard to the desired destination, the Algebra subfolder.

2. Copy multiple contiguous files.

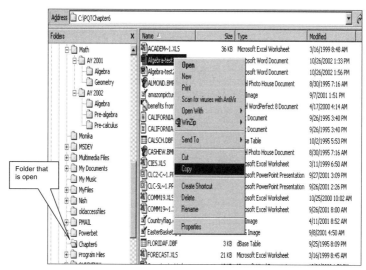

Figure 6.21.   Pop-Up Menu for <Right-Click> for a File

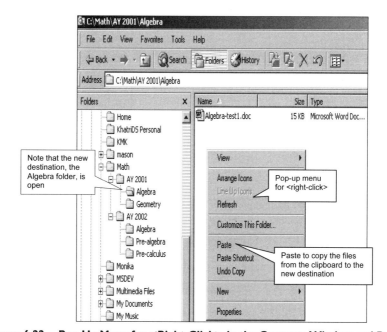

Figure 6.22.   Pop-Up Menu for <Right-Click> in the Contents Window and Paste

2.1. **Click** the source folder, Chapter6, again in the *Folders window* to open it.

2.2. **Click** in the column heading for Type to sort files by their file types.

2.3. **Click** the first Word file (file extension DOC, the three letters following the period in the filename. If the file extension is not displayed, identify Word files under the Type column and then select the filename under the Name column).

2.4. **Press** and **hold** the <shift> key and **click** on the third Word file. This will select three contiguous files that will have DOC as file extensions (figure 6.23).

2.5. **Click** the Copy icon in the *Toolbar*.

2.6. **Click** the Geometry subfolder under the *AY 2001 folder* to open it.

2.7. **Right-click** in the Contents window empty space and then **click** on Paste from the *pop-up menu*. The files are copied in the Geometry subfolder as shown in figure 6.24.

3. Practice in copying multiple noncontiguous files.

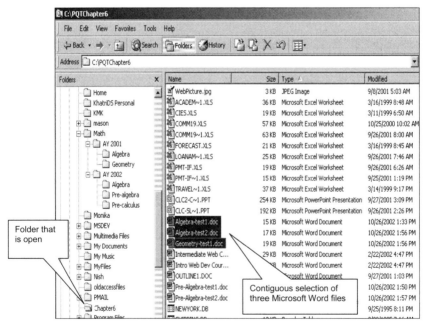

Figure 6.23.   Selection of Three Contiguous Word Files

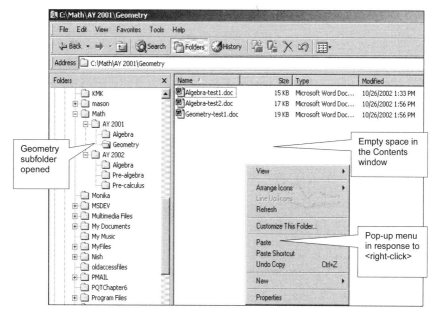

Figure 6.24. Three Contiguous MS Word Files Copied in the Geometry Subfolder

For groups: By this time, students have acquired enough knowledge in copying files. Ask students one at a time to give instructions aloud to other students for first selecting and then copying non-contiguous files. Dialogue 6.4 demonstrates the desired interaction between the teacher and students.

For individual readers: You have acquired enough knowledge to further practice your learning through the use of the dialogue session that follows.

TEACHER DIRECTED/INDIVIDUAL READER EXERCISES

1. Sort the contents of the Chapter6 in descending order by Filenames, Filetypes, Size, and Date Modified.
2. How many objects (files, folders, or both) are there in this folder? Hint: press <ctrl-A> to select all the contents of the folder.

Dialogue 6.4.   A Sample Dialogue Session for Selecting and Copying Noncontiguous Files

Below is an excerpt from an actual computer training session

Session Dialogue		Teaching Principles (*) Management Tactics (■) Illustrated
Teacher	Now, we want to select four files, one of each type, which probably will be non-contiguous. How do we select such files from the Chapter6 folder, Gene?	
Gene	First, **click** on the AY 2002 folder.	
Teacher	Are you sure? (*A student should first click on the source folder.*)	* ■ * ■
Helen	No. Maybe I should first click on the source folder, Chapter6.	
Teacher	Yes. The source folder must be opened first. Now, we have selected such a folder, how do we select four files, one of each type, Vinod?	Practice with learned concepts · Call students by name · Use inductive approach · Gain and maintain attention
Vinod	I should first **click** on the column heading Type to sort that column in alphabetical order. Then **click** on the first file of one type. **Press** the <Ctrl> key and keep it pressed, and then **click** on the three files that are of different types.	
Teacher	That is wonderful. (*This selection is shown in figure 6.25.*) Now, how do we copy this selection of files to the Pre-calculus sub-folder located under the AY 2002 folder, Cameron?	
Cameron	First, **copy** the files to the clipboard by right-clicking on the selection and then **clicking** on the Copy choice from the *pop-up menu.*	
Teacher	I like this. Now, how do we copy these files from the clipboard to the Pre-calculus subfolder under the AY 2002 folder, Tracy?	
Tracy	OK. I will try. First, **click** on the AY 2002 folder. Then you **right-click** in the Contents window. Next, you **click** on Paste in the *pop-up menu.*	
Teacher	You are doing very well. (*Four noncontiguous files, each one of them of a different type, are copied to the destination folder.*)	

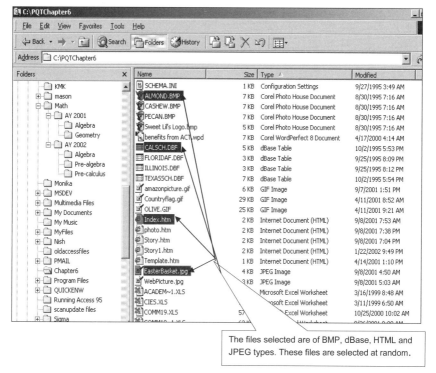

Figure 6.25.   Four Noncontiguous Randomly Selected Files in Chapter 6 Folder

3. You are an English teacher and are teaching writing and grammar to the ninth graders and composition and advanced writing to the twelfth graders during the first semester of 2004. Also, you are assigned to teach spelling and writing to the ninth graders and grammar and literature to the twelfth graders during the second semester of 2004. First, organize the folders on a piece of paper and then create all the necessary folders on the computer under the C: hard drive.

4. Select contiguous and noncontiguous files and copy them to appropriate folders you just created. Also, select all Word files and copy them in the Literature folders. In addition, select two Excel files and three HTML files and copy this selection to the ninth grade's writing folder.

7

ORGANIZATION OF COURSE MATERIAL: THE WONDERFUL WORLD OF WORD PROCESSING

Are there enough hours in a day to prepare for your teaching in each of your courses? Do you find yourself treating the students to samples of your handwriting more often than you like? Do the students react to these samples with such statements as, "What is the word at the end of the third line on the chalkboard?" "Is the number in the second question on the board a 7 or a 9?" From the back row, a querulous voice grumbles, "I can't read it because the writing is too small, too light." If you have been treated to these or similar statements in your classes or have experienced them with teachers you have had, then you need some help in the pedagogical techniques of precourse planning and management tactics.

Fortunately, there is an electronic good fairy available, known by the less than dazzling name of *word processor*. You, as a teacher, have to write; why not let the electronic good fairy help you?

This chapter is designed to assist you in carrying out three important categories of tasks: creating outlines, developing test materials of various types, and organizing information in computer files. Before we start creating these tasks, however, an introduction to a word processor is provided. For illustrative purposes, we have chosen Word 97 as the word processor.

BASICS OF MICROSOFT WORD 97

First off, a word processor is not synonymous with a typewriter. Many of us started out using a computer as a typewriter. This approach cuts the wings off the fairy. A word processor is really a magical tool, and we want you to learn it as a teaching aid.

Starting Word

1. **Double-click** the icon for <u>Microsoft Word</u> on the *Desktop* if one is already created. The system will display the Word Window as shown in figure 7.1. If you do not see the icon for Word on the desktop, then you need to follow the three steps next provided.
2. **Click** <u>Start</u> located on the extreme left of the *Taskbar*.
3. **Click** <u>Programs</u> in the *Start* menu.
4. **Click** <u>Microsoft Word</u> in the *Programs* menu.

<u>Note</u>: *Also, these three steps may be different on your computer depending on how a particular word processing program has been installed on*

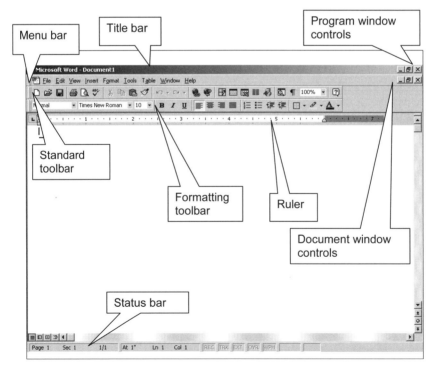

Figure 7.1.   Word 97 with Document, Program Window Controls, and Bars

it. If this is so, you will need to seek assistance before you can begin the rest of the chapter.

As soon as you open the Word program, you will see a computer window (shown in figure 7.1). Before you proceed further, you should memorize the different parts of the window and their locations.

Short Explanations of the Word Window's Parts

Title bar   The Title bar contains the program name, the current document name, and window controls. If the document has not been named, the default name, Document1, appears.

Menu bar   The Menu bar gives you access to all the features in Word. It consists of pull-down menus that contain commands needed to perform various Word operations.

Toolbars   By default, the Standard toolbar and the Formatting toolbar are located below the Menu bar and are used to quickly access the most commonly used Word features.

Status bar   The Status bar appears at the bottom of the application window. It informs you about the status of various Word features and about the document itself.

To review these explanations, we present dialogue 7.1 focused on identifying icons on the Standard and the Formatting toolbars. If you are an individual reader, complete the dialogue yourself.

Don't panic at all about these boxes you see in figure 7.2 and figure 7.3. We are just naming the icons with their specific functions for both the Standard and Formatting toolbars.

The difference between the New and Open icons must be clearly understood. The icon labeled New opens a blank new document. The icon labeled Open recalls an existing document (a document that has already been created earlier) to the screen.

HIDE AND UNHIDE TOOLBARS AND THE RULER

Many times, an inexperienced user will inadvertently hide the toolbars. When you open Word, you sometimes may find the toolbars missing. This may create a panic situation for you. To know what to do in a situation like

Dialogue 7.1. A Sample Dialogue Session for Toolbars and Their Icons

Below is an excerpt from an actual computer training session

Session Dialogue		Teaching Principles (*) Management Tactics (■) Illustrated
Teacher	Can you identify the Standard toolbar, Marcus?	
Marcus	Yes, the bar right under the Menu bar.	
Teacher	Good. Now can you identify the Formatting toolbar, Di?	* ■ * ■
Di	Yes, I can. The bar right under the Standard toolbar is the Formatting toolbar.	
Teacher	What does the first icon on the Standard toolbar signify, Dana?	
Dana	Looks like a blank piece of paper.	
Pat	It could be opening a new document.	
David	I know. It signifies "New."	
Teacher	How do you know this precise meaning, Brad?	
Brad	I just happened to point the mouse to this first icon. The computer shows the word New in yellow.	
Teacher	What does the next icon on the Standard toolbar signify, Todd?	
Todd	Open.	
Teacher	How do you know, Omar?	
Omar	I pointed the mouse to the second icon and the computer displays the word Open. (*It means opening an existing document. This pattern was followed until every student got a chance to tell the precise meaning of some of the more relevant icons in Word for both the Standard and Formatting toolbars.*)	

Right column vertical labels: Gain and maintain attention · Use inductive approach · Call students by name · Students participated in their learning

this is very important, so we are going to show you how to hide and then unhide toolbars, including the Ruler.

Hide Toolbars and Ruler

1. **Click** <u>View</u> in the *Menu* bar.
2. **Click** <u>Toolbars</u> ▶ in the *View* menu.
3. **Click** <u>Standard</u> from the list (figure 7.4). This will hide the Standard Toolbar.

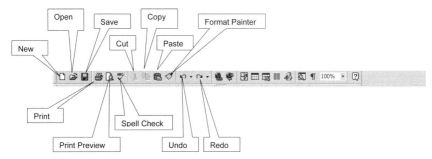

Figure 7.2. Functions of the Commonly Used Computer Icons of the Standard Toolbar

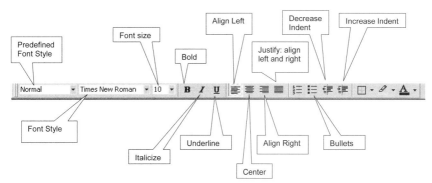

Figure 7.3. Functions of the Commonly Used Computer Icons of the Formatting Toolbar

4. **Click** View/Toolbars/Formatting to hide the Formatting Toolbar.
5. **Click** View/Ruler to hide the Ruler.

Unhide the Toolbars

A dialogue session is presented in dialogue 7.2 for unhiding the Toolbars.

OUTLINE A COURSE SYLLABUS

Open Word97 Program and Input Text

1. **Double-click** the icon for Word on the *Desktop*.
2. Type information as shown in figure 7.5. The text you type will even-

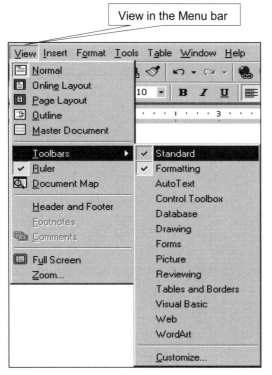

Figure 7.4.   Displaying Toolbars and the Ruler

tually be converted to a three-level numeric outline that can become part of a syllabus.

3. **Click** File in the *Menu* bar.
4. **Click** Save As . . . on the *File* menu. This is to save a file for the first time.
5. **Click** the <down-arrow> for the *Save in* objects box to select a folder where the file is to be saved.
6. **Click** the C: Drive.
7. **Double-click** the Chapter7 folder.
8. **Type** an appropriate name in the Filename text box (e.g., Course-Objectives). Precaution: If there is an old name in the Filename text box, delete it first. Then type the new name (figure 7.6).
9. **Click** Save to save the document. The document has now been saved under the name, Course-Objectives, in the Chapter7 folder.

Dialogue 7.2. "Unhiding" Toolbars in Word

Below is an excerpt from an actual computer training session

Session Dialogue		Teaching Principles (*) Management Tactics (■) Illustrated
Teacher	How will you get the Standard toolbar back, Pam?	* ■ * ■
Pam	Just undo what we just did for hiding the toolbars.	Students participated in their learning / Call students by name / Use inductive approach / Gain and maintain attention
Teacher	Can you walk us through the steps for un-hiding the Standard toolbar, Scott?	
Scott	Sure. **Click** on View/Toolbars/Standard.	
Teacher	How do we unhide the Formatting toolbar, Tara?	
Tara	**Click** on View/Toolbars/Formatting.	
	(If the trainer wishes, this pattern can be followed for the Ruler and the Drawing Toolbar. The individual reader can also follow the same pattern.)	

COURSE OBJECTIVES
Introduction to College Physics

The major goal of the course is to tie all of the physical quantities (topics) and their respective units to everyday daily experiences with the major emphasis on problem solving.

Teacher Academic Objectives
Define physical quantities
Provide units of physical quantities
Provide emphasis on problem solving to take fear out of "word problem-solving"

Teacher Pedagogical Objectives
Provide practice in writing
Provide clear definitions
Identify given and unknown quantities in problem solving
Prepare all tests/exams based on classroom notes
Grade strictly on performance (not on a predetermined grade distribution)

Attention-getting Objectives
Spoil not less than three weekends
Maintain zero nap taking in class

Figure 7.5. Text to Be Typed for an Exercise by a User in Word

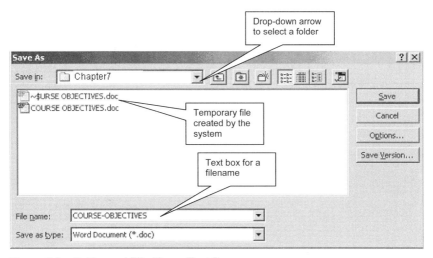

Figure 7.6. Folder and File Name Text Boxes

Formatting Text for Appearance

1. **Select** the first heading of the text. One way of doing it is to click in the beginning of text and then drag to the end of it. The selected text is shown as highlighted (figure 7.7).
2. **Click** the icon for <u>Center</u> in the *Formatting* toolbar to center the selected text.
3. **Click** the icon for <u>Bold</u> in the *Formatting* toolbar to bold the selected text.
4. **Select** subheading of the text.
5. **Click** the icon for <u>Center</u> in the *Formatting* toolbar to center the selected text.
6. **Click** the icon for <u>Italic</u> in the *Formatting* toolbar to italicize the selected text.
7. **Click** in the beginning of the first paragraph and **press** the <u>Tab</u> key. (This will move [tab] the first line of the paragraph to the right.) The results of this formatting are shown in figure 7.8.

Figure 7.7. A Highlighted (Selected) Text

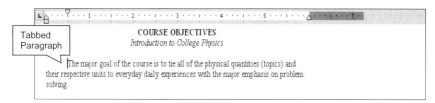

Figure 7.8.   Formatting Changes in Response to the Previous Commands

8. **Use** the <backspace> key to delete the Tab previously inserted.
9. **Click** on the icon for Increase Indent in the *Formatting* toolbar. The results of the indentation are shown in figure 7.9. (This will move [indent] the entire paragraph to the right.)

Create a Multilevel Numeric (Legal) Outline

1. **Select** the text starting from Teacher Academic Objectives to the end of the document (figure 7.10).
2. **Click** Format in the *Menu* bar and then on Bullets and Numbering . . . in the *Format* menu as shown above. The system will display figure 7.11.
3. **Click** the tab for Outline Numbered.
4. **Click** on the display box for Numeric (Legal Outline) and then **Click**> OK. The system creates a first-level outline for the selected text as shown in figure 7.12.
5. Now **select** lines marked as 2, 3, and 4.
6. **Press** the <Tab> key. The system creates a second level of the outline for the selected items as shown in figure 7.13.
7. **Select** newly marked 3 through 7 lines.

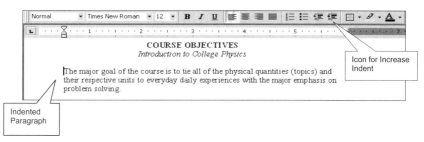

Figure 7.9.   Formatted with Indentation

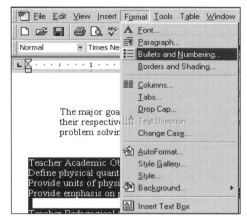

Figure 7.10. Selection for Creating Outline

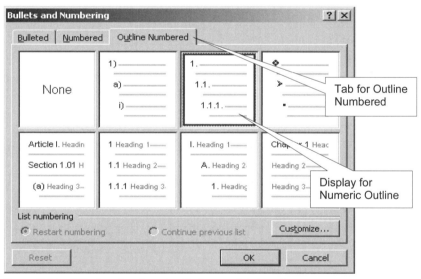

Figure 7.11. Window for Creating Bullets and Other Outlines

1. Teacher Academic Objectives
2. Define physical quantities
3. Provide units of physical quantities
4. Provide emphasis on problem solving to take fear out of "word problem-solving"

5. Teacher Pedagogical Objectives
6. Provide practice in writing
7. Provide clear definitions
8. Identify given and unknown quantities in problem solving
9. Prepare all tests/exams based on classroom notes
10. Grade strictly on performance (not on a predetermined grade distribution)

11. Attention-getting Objectives
12. Spoil not less than three weekends
13. Maintain zero nap taking in class

Figure 7.12.   First-Level Numeric Outline

The major goal of the course is to tie all of the physical quantities (topics) and their respective units to everyday daily experiences with the major emphasis on problem solving.

1. Teacher Academic Objectives
   1.1   Define physical quantities
   1.2   Provide units of physical quantities
   1.3   Provide emphasis on problem solving to take fear out of "word problem-solving" |

2. Teacher Pedagogical Objectives
3. Provide practice in writing
4. Provide clear definitions
5. Identify given and unknown quantities in problem solving
6. Prepare all tests/exams based on classroom notes
7. Grade strictly on performance (not on a predetermined grade distribution)

8. Attention-getting Objectives
9. Spoil not less than three weekends
10. Maintain zero nap taking in class

Figure 7.13.   Second-Level Outline Created for the First Objective

8. **Press** the <u>Tab</u> key. The system this time creates a second-level outline for the selected items as shown in figure 7.14.

Now, it's your turn to fix the rest of the outline (dialogue 7.3).

Once the dialogue session is correctly completed, you will see the following three-level outline as shown in figure 7.15.

We have walked you through the process of creating an outline, but for

1. Teacher Academic Objectives
   1.1   Define physical quantities
   1.2   Provide units of physical quantities
   1.3   Provide emphasis on problem solving to take fear out of "word problem-solving"

2. Teacher Pedagogical Objectives
   2.1   Provide practice in writing
   2.2   Provide clear definitions
   2.3   Identify given and unknown quantities in problem solving
   2.4   Prepare all tests/exams based on classroom notes
   2.5   Grade strictly on performance (not on a predetermined grade distribution)

3. Attention-getting Objectives
4. Spoil not less than three weekends
5. Maintain zero nap taking in class

Figure 7.14. Second-Level Outline Created for the Second Objective

Dialogue 7.3.   A Sample Dialogue Session for Completing the Three-Level Outline

Below is an excerpt from an actual computer training session

Session Dialogue		Teaching Principles (*) Management Tactics (■) Illustrated
Teacher	How do we create a second-order outline for items marked as 4 and 5, Vivienne?	* ■ * ■
Vivienne	**Select** current items 4 and 5 and **press** the <Tab> key.	Gain and maintain attention — Use inductive approach — Call students by name — Students participated in their learning
Teacher	Well done. Now, how do create a third-level outline for items marked as 2.2 and 2.3, Erick?	
Erick	**Select** items 2.2 and 2.3, and **press** the <Tab> key.	
Teacher	Very good. (*The outcome of this dialogue is shown in figure 7.15.*)	

COURSE OBJECTIVES
Introduction to College Physics

The major goal of the course is to tie all of the physical quantities (topics) and their respective units to everyday daily experiences with the major emphasis on problem solving.

1. Teacher Academic Objectives
    1.1 Define physical quantities
    1.2 Provide units of physical quantities
    1.3 Provide emphasis on problem solving to take fear out of "word problem-solving"

2. Teacher Pedagogical Objectives
    2.1 Provide practice in writing
        2.1.1 Provide clear definitions
        2.1.2 Identify given and unknown quantities in problem solving
    2.2 Prepare all tests/exams based on classroom notes
    2.3 Grade strictly on performance (not on a predetermined grade distribution)

3. Attention-getting Objectives
    3.1 Spoil not less than three weekends
    3.2 Maintain zero nap taking in class

Figure 7.15. Completed Three-Level Outline after the Dialogue Session

you to master it, you will need to practice, practice, and then practice some more. You thought you were off the hook for the outline? Forget it. At the end of this chapter, as an honor, you will be creating a three-level outline again.

CREATING A CLASS TEST

The sample test created here contains questions from different disciplines. The emphasis is *not* on the content of the test, but rather on the techniques that are available in Word to create tests in various formats. The techniques that are introduced show the power of the word processor. Brace yourself!

Typing Straight Text for a Test

1. **Type** information as presented in figure 7.16. Here are the instructions.

Sample Tests' Questions from Different Disciplines

Answer All Questions

1. In a television tube, electrons are emitted from an electrode at one end of the tube and strike a
    light-emitting coating on the picture screen at the other end of the tube. If the electrons are
    emitted with a velocity of 1.5×10^8 m/s, how long does it take the electrons to hit the screen that
    is 0.20 m away?
2. Identify the reactants and products in each of the following reaction equations:

    $H2 + Cl2 \rightarrow 2HCL$

3. Solve for the unknown quantity.

4. What are the three branches of the U.S. government?
5. VA, DC, and MD
6. Judiciary, Legislative, and Executive
7. Virginia, Legislative Assembly, and local governments
8. Supreme Court, House of Representatives, President
9. All of the above

Figure 7.16.   Text for a Sample Test from Various Disciplines

1.1. Starting with question 1, type a number one followed by a pe-
      riod (1.) and then **press** the <Tab> key before you start typing
      text. After typing the text for question 1, **press** the <Enter>
      key. This will automatically generate the number 2 for the sec-
      ond question.
1.2. The right-arrow in the chemistry reaction equation (question 2)
      is inserted by **clicking** first on Insert in the *Menu* bar and then
      on *Symbol* in the *Insert* menu. To complete the insertion of the
      right-arrow, follow the directions in the Symbol's window.

Also, when typing, don't press the <Enter> key until you are finished with
the question. That gives the question numbers automatically. To insert extra
spaces as shown between some questions, press the <Enter> key after clicking the cursor at the end of each question. If you end up with an extra question
number, use the <backspace> key to delete that question number.

Note: Items 5 through 9 will be converted eventually into a two-level
outline in the typical format of multiple-choice test items.

Never be afraid of saving a document. *It is a lifesaver.* Saving often elimi-
nates the frustration and anxiety that comes with the use of a computer. A

dialogue that provides practice in saving a document for the first time is provided in dialogue 7.4.

Create Superscripts

1. **Select** number 8 only in the *third line* of question 1 (figure 7.16).
2. **Click** Format in the *Menu* bar. The Format menu is displayed (figure 7.18).
3. **Click** Font . . . in the *Format* menu. The Font dialogue box appears (figure 7.19).
4. **Click** in the check box for Superscript under the *Effects* section.
5. **Click** OK. The number 8 is now shown in superscript (figure 7.20).

Dialogue 7.4. A Sample Dialogue Session in Saving a File for the First Time

Below is an excerpt from an actual computer training session

Session Dialogue		Teaching Principles (*) Management Tactics (■) Illustrated
Teacher	At this stage, we want to save this file in the Chapter7 folder under a filename Test1. How do we go about it, Amie?	■ Gain and maintain attention * Use inductive approach ■ Call students by name * Students participated in their learning * Reinforcement of concepts learned earlier
Amie	**Click** File in the *Menu bar* and **click** on Save As . . . in the *File* menu.	
Teacher	What do we do next, Cynthia?	
Cynthia	**Select** the Chapter7 folder from the drop-down list in the *Save In* text box.	
Teacher	Good. Is there anything else we need to do, Fitsum?	
Fitsum	Yes. **Type** a new filename, Test1, in *the File Name text box*, and then **click** on Save.	
Teacher	We are getting to the end. Let us do some formatting changes. How will we center and bold the first line in this test, Khesha?	
Khesha	First, **select** the first line and then **press** the Center icon in the *Formatting toolbar.*	
Teacher	We are almost to the finish line. Now, the last thing. How will we italicize the second line, Michael?	
Michael	**Select** the second line and then **press** the Italic icon in the *Formatting toolbar.*	
Teacher	We are doing wonders with this exercise. *(The output of these formatting changes is shown in figure 7.17.)*	

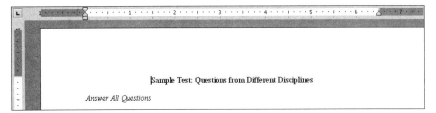

Figure 7.17.   Formatted Text as a Result of Centering, Bolding, and Italicizing

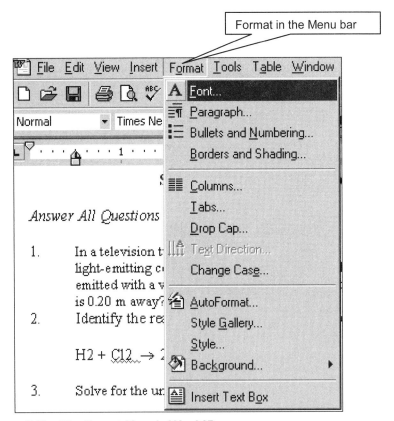

Figure 7.18.   The Format Menu in Word 97

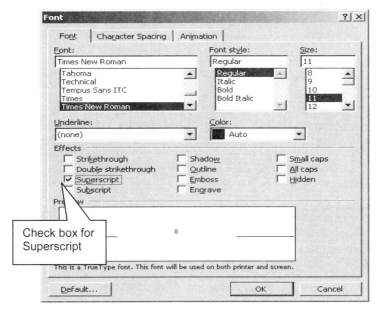

Figure 7.19.   The Font Dialog Box for Adjusting Formatting

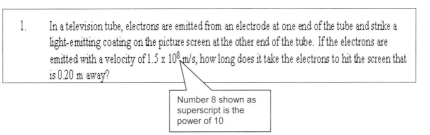

Figure 7.20.   The Number 8 Shown as a Superscript

Create Subscripts

1. **Select** the number 2 in H2 only in Question #2.
2. **Click** Format in the *Menu* bar.
3. **Click** Font . . . in the *Format* menu.
4. **Click** in the check box for Subscript under the *Effects* section, and **Click** OK. The number 2 will now appear as a subscript.
5. Repeat the subscripting steps for the number 2 in Cl2. The output for these actions is shown in figure 7.21.

> 2.   Identify the reactants and products in each of the following reaction equations:
>
> $H_2 + Cl_2 \rightarrow 2HCl$

Figure 7.21.   The Subscripted Chemistry Equation

Authors' Note: Take a break. Get a latte. Misery is about to happen.

Create Math Equations

1. **Click** in the empty space between questions 3 and 4.
2. **Click** Insert in the *Menu* bar. The Format menu appears, as shown in figure 7.22.
3. **Click** Object . . . in the *Format* menu. The Object dialogue window appears as shown in figure 7.23.

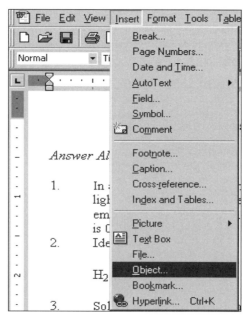

Figure 7.22.   Getting Ready to Insert a Math Equation

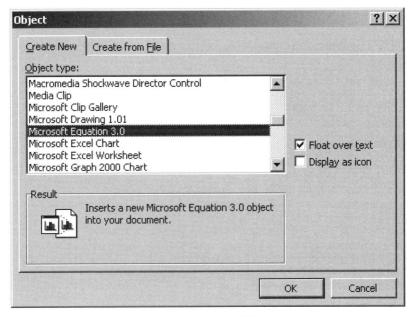

Figure 7.23. Selecting Microsoft Equation 3.0 Object

Caution: If the option for Microsoft Equation 3.0 is not listed, then it is not installed on your computer and you need to install it before you can proceed any further.

4. **Click** the tab for Create New in the *Object* window.

5. **Click** Microsoft Equation 3.0 in the list and **click** OK. The system will display an Equation toolbar and an Equation object as shown in figure 7.24.

6. **Click** the symbol for Fraction and radical templates in the *Equation* toolbar. A set of eleven templates is displayed by the system as shown in figure 7.25.

7. **Click** the first figure in the *top left-hand corner* (the first template). As a result of this action, the first template appears by itself in an enlarged form (figure 7.26).

8. **Type** X in the *numerator*; **click** in the denominator placeholder and **type** 5.

$$\frac{X}{5}$$

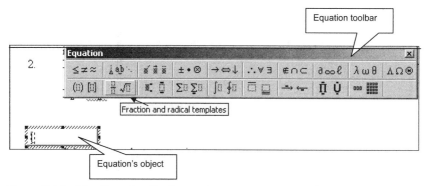

Figure 7.24.   The Equation Toolbar and the Equation's Object

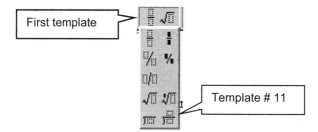

Figure 7.25.   Eleven Fraction and Radical Templates in Word 97

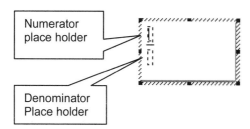

Figure 7.26.   First of the Eleven Fraction and Radical Templates in Word 97

9. **Click** to the right of this expression you just typed besides the dash.
10. **Type** an equal sign (=). The result is shown below. Keep the cursor right there. Now, you are going to repeat the previous five steps for the right side of the equal (=) sign.

$$\frac{X}{5} =$$

11. **Click** again the icon for Fraction and radical templates in the *Equation* toolbar.
12. **Click** the first template in the *top left-hand corner*. (Notice that the cursor is now to the right of the equal sign.)
13. **Type** 20 in the *numerator* placeholder, **click** in the denominator placeholder, and **type** X.
14. **Close** the Equation toolbar. Your work will now show the completed equation as shown below.

$$\frac{X}{5} = \frac{20}{X}$$

The math equation should appear in your document as an Equation box as shown above. If it doesn't, you may have to resize the Equation box and move it to an appropriate place to fit the rest of the problem.

Becoming proficient on this task is a pain. However, once you have done the work and have lived through it, the equations are reusable and will save you a lot of work over the long haul.

Create a Multiple Choice Outline

1. **Select** items labeled 5 through 9 as shown in figure 7.27.
2. **Click** Format in the *Menu* bar.

Authors' Note: "Do we hear an incredulous, 'I don't believe it'?" Cheer up. Don't give up. Even, we, the authors, took a break here when we were editing this section. Hang in, we're almost to the finish line.

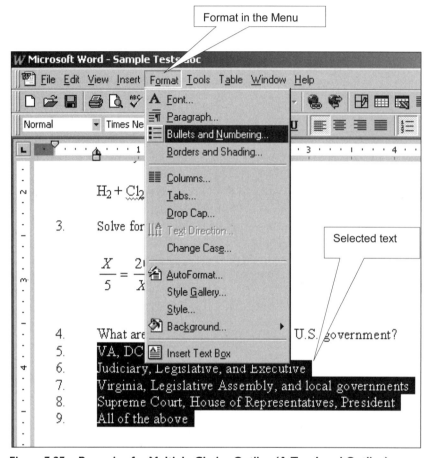

Figure 7.27.   Preparing for Multiple-Choice Outline (A Two-Level Outline)

3. **Click** Bullets and Numbering . . . in the *Format* menu. The Bullets and Numbering dialog box appears as shown in figure 7.28.
4. **Click** the tab for *Outline Numbered*.
5. **Click** the second choice in the *first* row.
6. **Click** Restart numbering in the *List Numbering* section.
7. **Click** on the Customize . . . pushbutton. The window for customized Outline Numbered List will appear in response to this action. Check the settings for two (2) under Level and make necessary changes for Aligned at: and Indent at: as shown in figure 7.29.
8. **Click** OK.

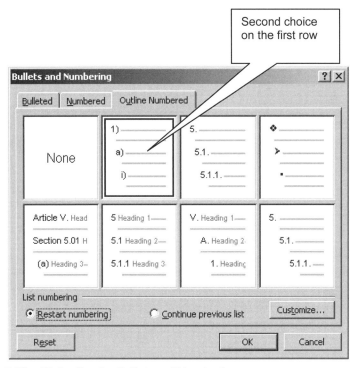

Figure 7.28. Dialog Box for Bullets and Numbering

9. **Press** the <u>Tab</u> key when the text is still selected (true in Word 97). Don't deselect the text. If you inadvertently deselect the text, select it again and then press the <Tab> key. The output of these actions in the form of a multiple-choice question is shown in figure 7.30.

   Note: Items like these can also be done in numeric outline. The steps for doing this outline may not be the same in Word 2000.

ORGANIZING INFORMATION IN A TABLE

Many times, you need to organize information in a tabular form for ease of reading, clarity of data presentation, creating an impressive presentation, preparing a professional article, or just plain dazzling your students with your expertise in this area. In any case, you need to create a table with a

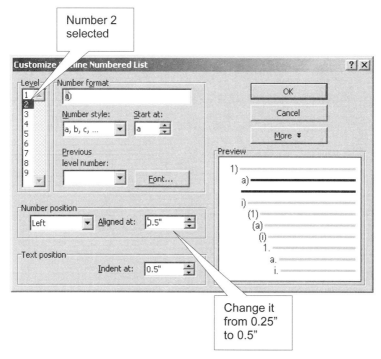

Number 2 selected

Change it from 0.25" to 0.5"

Figure 7.29.   Dialog Window for Customized Outline Numbered List

4.   What are the three branches of the U.S. government?
    a) VA, DC, and MD
    b) Judiciary, Legislative, and Executive
    c) Virginia, Legislative Assembly, and local governments
    d) Supreme Court, House of Representatives, President
    e) All of the above

Figure 7.30.   The Last Question in the Multiple-Choice Form

certain number of rows and columns. The rows are arranged horizontally while the columns are displayed in a vertical fashion.

Inserting an Empty Table

1. **Click** on Table in the *Menu* bar. The Table menu is displayed.
2. **Click** the Insert table . . . choice in the Table menu. The Insert Table dialog window is displayed, as shown in figure 7.31.
3. **Change** the number of columns to five (5) and the number of rows to seven (7) as shown in figure 7.32.
4. **Click** OK to complete this action. The system will insert a table with five columns each of width 1.2"and seven rows as shown below when the left and right margins are set at 1.25" (figure 7.33). If these margins are not set for 1.25", the width of columns will be different.

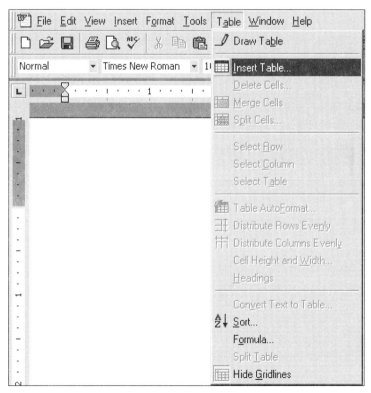

Figure 7.31. Table Menu for Creating a Table for the First Time

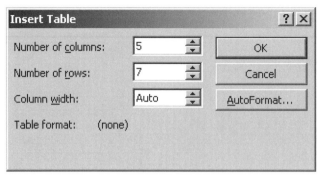

Figure 7.32. Specifying Number of Rows and Columns for a Table

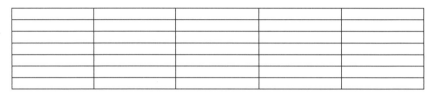

Figure 7.33. An Empty Table with Five Equidistant Columns and Seven Rows

Resize Table Columns

1. **Click** anywhere in the *table*, but do not select a cell. If a cell is highlighted, it is selected. To deselect a cell, click once anywhere else in the table.
2. **Bring** the pointer near the boundary separating the columns. The pointer will change into a double-headed horizontal arrow with a vertical solid line or two vertical fine lines. When that happens, click and hold the click and then move the pointer either to the left or right to change the column width.
3. **Change** the widths of columns 1, 2, 4, and 5 to approximately 1.00" and of column 3 to about 2.00" by using the technique described in the previous step. When these steps are all done, your empty table will look like the one shown in figure 7.34.

Type and Format Text in a Table

1. **Type** information as shown in figure 7.35.
   Precaution: Do not press the <Enter> key to move from cell to cell

Figure 7.34.   A Table with 1″ Width for Columns 1, 2, 4, and 5 and 2″ Width for Column 3

Tests/Exams	Chapters	Description	Scheduled Date	Return Date
1	1, 2, 3, 4	Four problems with parts and two bonus questions	9/23/02	9/25/02
2	5, 6, 7, 8	Four problems with parts and one bonus question	10/21/02	10/23/02
3	9, 10, 11	Three problems and two bonus questions	11/18/02	11/20/02
4	12, 13, 14, 15	Three problems and one bonus question	12/16/02	12/18/02

Figure 7.35.   Test Schedule from a Physics Syllabus Organized in Tabular Form

in a table. Instead, use the <Tab> key to move between cells. You can also click in a cell to move to that cell.

Add or Delete Rows or Columns

1. **Click** inside a cell where you want to insert or delete a row or a column.
2. **Right-click** in the cell.
3. **Click** Insert Rows in the *Pop-up* menu to insert rows before the current row (figure 7.36). To insert a row at the end of a table, click in the last cell of the table, and then press the <Tab> key. To delete a row, select the row first. Then <right-click> in the selected row and click Delete Rows in the pop-up menu.

For example, when a row is deleted, the system will show you an updated table without the deleted row. Let us see if you can help me do some formatting in the table (dialogue 7.5).

Figure 7.36.   Inserting Rows in a Word Table

Note: *You must complete this dialogue session before moving on to the next section or chapter to observe what is shown in figure 7.35.*
As we noted earlier with the outline, you will need to practice and practice. Then you will need to practice some more to become truly proficient in creating tables.

❂   ❂   ❂   ❂   ❂

TRAINER DIRECTED/INDIVIDUAL READER EXERCISES

1. First, write a three-level outline for the three branches of government, their various branches and/or offices in longhand. Then, create the same three-level outline in a word processor.
2. Create a test with math, science, and multiple-choice questions.
3. Create a roster in tabular form of the class attendees in a word processor.

Dialogue 7.5.   A Sample Dialogue Session in Formatting Text in a Table and Saving a File

Below is an excerpt from an actual computer training session

Session Dialogue		Teaching Principles (*) Management Tactics (■) Illustrated
Teacher	At this stage, we would like to format some of the text in the table. How do we bold the text in the column headings, Todd?	
Todd	What is a column heading?	* * ■ * ■
Teacher	Usually the text typed in row 1 across the columns. Now, can you answer the question raised earlier, Keyonna?	Reinforcement of concepts learned earlier · Students participated in their learning · Call students by name · Use inductive approach · Gain and maintain attention
Keyonna	Yes, I can. **Select** all column headings (*row 1*) and then **Click** on the Bold icon in the *Formatting toolbar.*	
Teacher	How nice. Now, how can we center the tests/exams numbers in column one.	
Deena	No big deal. Just select items 1, 2, 3, 4 in column 1 and then **Click** on the Center icon in the *Formatting toolbar.*	
Teacher	We are doing well so far. There is just one more thing we must do before taking a break. Can someone read my mind?	
Students	Sure. You want us to tell you how we save this work.	
Teacher	Absolutely. How do you propose that we save this work in the Chapter7 folder and assign a name, Exam Schedule, Tinh?	
Tinh	Very easy. **Click** on File in the *Menu bar.* **Click** on Save as. **Change** the folder to Chapter7 and then **type** the Exam Schedule for the *File name.* Finally, **click** Save.	
Teacher	This is just great. (*The output of these formatting changes is shown in figure 7.35.*)	

8

ELECTRONIC GRADE BOOK

Most teachers consider the recording of student grades for various tests, papers, and projects on a course-by-course basis to be a swift pain. And some teachers spend hours upon hours finalizing grades for their students. Other teachers out of desperation quasi-wing it, assign a grade, and hope nobody complains. Is any one of these types resonating with you? It becomes even harder for a college professor trying to locate the record of a student who took one course, maybe seven—or was it six?—years ago, and wants a letter of recommendation for graduate school. Even in the electronic age, most teachers are still preparing their grade books manually. Think about it. You have been—or will be—hired to teach students, not to be an example of a nineteenth-century file clerk. "All right," you grumble. "So, what's the solution?" And we heave a sigh of relief and say, "We thought you'd never ask." There really is an easy way to eliminate this pain, and it will move you in the blink of an eye from the nineteenth to the twenty-first century. The solution is contained in using a spreadsheet for electronic grading and record keeping.

So, what do you need to learn? Just have patience; we will take you there.

The chapter is divided into four sections: becoming familiar with a spreadsheet, creating a one-year grade book, creating a multiyear grade book, and searching for information in a consolidated grade book that contains multiple years and courses. In this chapter, we will use the Excel 97 spreadsheet program.

BECOMING FAMILIAR WITH A SPREADSHEET

A spreadsheet is composed of columns and rows. The columns in Excel 97 are labeled with the English alphabet or combinations of this alphabet's letters (e.g., A, B, AA, AB, BA, BB, IA, IB, etc.). The rows are labeled with numbers: 1, 2, 3, and so on. The intersection of a row and a column defines a cell. For example, the cell labeled as A1 is in column A and row 1. In contrast, cell B5 is in column B, row 5. This pattern is followed throughout.

Excel 97 is a program that creates a three-dimensional spreadsheet called a book. And like a book, it has multiple pages or sheets. Thus, a book in Excel 97 refers to many sheets of paper (of which only three are shown here). Each sheet has a total of 256 (2^8) columns and 65,536 (2^{16}) rows. Other sheets can be added or deleted, and the names of every sheet can be changed if desired. So you can have as many sheets as you want.

Starting Excel 97 Program

1. **Double-click** the icon for Excel on the *Desktop* if one is already created for you. If no icon is present, then follow the next three steps.
2. **Click** Start button in the *Taskbar* in the lower left corner of the Desktop.
3. **Click** Programs in the *Start* menu.
4. **Click** Excel.

The system will display figure 8.1 for Excel 97. For ease of referencing, various parts of this screen are labeled.

You must memorize the names of various parts of this screen before proceeding further. If you don't, you will be up the proverbial creek with no paddles.

Excel 97 Standard Toolbar

An Excel 97 Standard toolbar with its various icons marked with text is shown in figure 8.2. The actual name of an icon can also be ascertained by pointing the mouse to that icon, but don't click.

Excel 97 Formatting Toolbar

An Excel 97 Formatting toolbar with its various icons marked with text is shown in figure 8.3. The actual name of an icon can also be ascertained by pointing the mouse to that icon, but don't click.

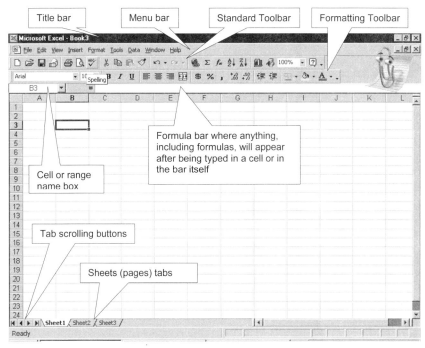

Figure 8.1. Excel 97 Main Screen with Various Parts

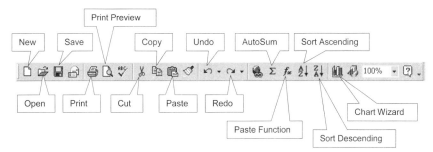

Figure 8.2. Icon Names for Standard Toolbar in Excel 97

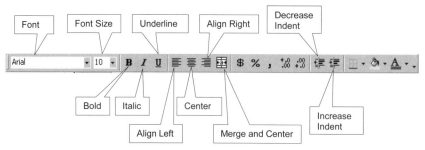

Figure 8.3. Icon Names for Formatting Toolbar in Excel 97

Mouse Pointer Positions

The mouse pointer in Excel 97 can take three different positions in a selected cell (figure 8.4).

Select position. The mouse pointer is in the select position when it takes the shape of a thick white cross. It is observed when the mouse pointer is positioned *inside* a selected cell. You must select a cell or a set of cells before you can take any other action(s) on the selected cell(s).

Copying position. The mouse pointer changes to a thin black cross (also known as *fill handle* position) when the pointer is positioned towards the *bottom right corner* of a selected cell. You must wait for the thin black cross to appear before you can start copying.

Move position. The mouse pointer changes to an arrow. This change will be observed when you position the mouse pointer toward the *boundary of a selected cell*. The exception is the bottom right corner, which is the copying position.

Authors' Note: We hate to sound like a broken record, but this set of actions requires the pedagogical technique of practice, practice, and more practice. Otherwise, you will once again be up that proverbial creek with no paddles.

Before taking any one of these actions (selecting, copying, moving), position the mouse and wait for the mouse pointer to change to one of the three shapes before clicking and dragging.

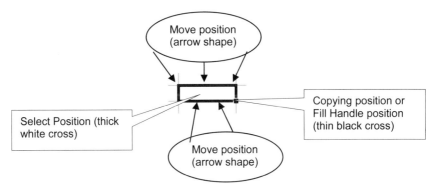

Figure 8.4. Mouse Pointer in Three Positions in a Selected Cell

When you select more than one cell, one of the cells in this range may not seem to be highlighted, but it really is included as part of the selection.

Four Types of Information in an Excel Spreadsheet

To summarize, an Excel spreadsheet accepts four types of information: numbers, labels, formulas, and functions (dialogue 8.1).

The introduction to the Excel spreadsheet is now over since the exercises have been purely for practice. **Close** the Excel book without saving changes. Don't close the Excel program.

PREAMBLE TO AN ELECTRONIC GRADE BOOK

Sooner or later, you will be asked to assist in planning a student event. Here is an opportunity to dazzle your colleagues, your student committee, as well as the school administration. This planning will involve not only the logistics but also a budget. Your task here is to prepare the budget request for the school administration for an evening party for ninth and tenth graders. The request to the school should include all expenses and donations expected from students and parents in those two grades. Learning the techniques described here is preparatory to the tasks that follow.

Using a Customized Budget Template

1. Open a new Excel book by **Clicking** the icon for <u>New</u> in the *Standard* toolbar. This is only necessary if you have closed all the Excel books before this step and the Excel screen is dark gray.

Dialogue 8.1.   A Dialogue Session for Entering Four Types of Information in a Spreadsheet

Below is an excerpt from an actual computer training session

Session Dialogue		Teaching Principles (*) Management Tactics (■) Illustrated
Teacher	**Type** 5 in cell A1 and 11 in cell A2. **Press** the <Enter> key after typing each number. Now, select both cells A1 and A2. The selection will be as shown.  Although it appears that cell A1 is not selected, it really is. Move the cursor to the copying position. **Click** and **drag** it to cell A10. (*The system fills cells A3 to A10 with some numbers.*)	
		<div style="writing-mode: vertical-rl">* * ■ * ■ Students learn new concepts hands-on Students participated in their learning Call students by name Use inductive approach Gain and maintain attention</div>
	A table showing column A and B with rows 1–11: A1=5, A2=11, A3=17, A4=23, A5=29, A6=35, A7=41, A8=47, A9=53, A10=59	
Teacher	Can you explain these numbers, Alex?	
Alex	I haven't the faintest idea.	
Hope	The numbers look to be in some order, but I can't see why they are that way.	
Richard	I think I got it. The numbers in cells A3 to A10 are incremented by 6.	
Anthony	The number 6, I think, is coming from the difference between 11 in cell A2 and 5 in cell A1.	
Teacher	That is really good. You just have numbers in these cells (*First type of information*). The numbers form a series starting with 5 and	

ending with 59 with an increment of 6. Now **type** January in cell C1 and **press** the <Enter> key. **Click** back in cell C1. **Position** the Mouse pointer to the copying position and **click** and **drag** it to cell C12.

	A	B	C	D
1	5		January	
2	11		February	
3	17		March	
4	23		April	
5	29		May	
6	35		June	
7	41		July	
8	47		August	
9	53		September	
10	59		October	
11			November	
12			December	
13				

These are called labels in a spreadsheet (*Second type of information*). Can you explain these results, Oscar?

Oscar	Looks like the computer is very smart. It fills the entire series and sure beats typing all the names for the months.
Teacher	**Click** in cell B1 and **type** =A1+A2+A3+A4+A5+A6+A7+A8+A9+A10 and **press** the <Enter> key after typing this formula. (*Third type of information. A formula begins with an equal [=] sign*). What do you observe in cell B1, Amanda?
Amanda	I have a number 320 in cell B1, but it takes too long to type the formula without making any mistakes. Is there any short cut to it?
Teacher	Let us ask someone else in the class, Angelic?
Angelic	There has to be one, but I don't know what it is.
Teacher	Let's try something else to get the answer of 320.
Students	OK
Teacher	**Click** in cell A11. Now **click** on the AutoSum icon in the *Standard toolbar*, and then **press** the <Enter> key. Did you get an answer of 320, Chigo?
Chigo	Yes. But how did it happen?

Dialogue 8.1. (Continued)

Session Dialogue		Teaching Principles (*) Management Tactics (■) Illustrated
Teacher	Let's now look at the formula in the Formula bar. The system has inserted a Sum function in cell A11. The function, just like the formula, starts with an equal (=) sign and then uses the function name, SUM. The functions use open and close parentheses. The text within the parentheses is called the argument of the function. In this case, the cells to be added are A1 through A10. The colon (:) is the sign for the range. (A *function is the fourth type of information that a spreadsheet will accept.*)	

2. **Click** Open icon in the *Standard* toolbar.
3. **Change** the folder to Chapter8 (figure 8.5).
4. **Select** the file named Budget Request.
5. **Click** Open. The system brings a template on the screen to work with as shown in figure 8.6.
6. **Type** the budget numbers in the cells as shown in figure 8.7, **pressing** the <Enter> key after each entry.

Using Excel Functions and Formulas

If you are the teacher, you should continue with this style of dialogue with students for formatting cells, if possible (dialogue 8.2).

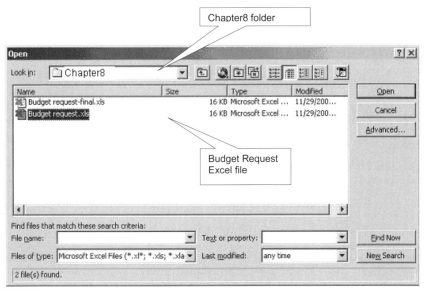

Figure 8.5. Opening an Excel File from the Chapter 8 Folder

Formatting Cells

Formatting is required to enhance the appearance and layout of a spreadsheet.

1. **Select** cells A6 and A7.
2. **Click** Increase Indent icon and then on the Italic icon in *Formatting* toolbar.
3. **Select** cells A12 through A18.
4. **Click** Increase Indent icon and then on the Italic icon in *Formatting* toolbar.
5. **Select** cells A1 through D3.
6. **Click** *Format* in the Menu bar and then Cells . . . in the *Format* menu.
7. **Click** tab for Alignment.
8. **Select** Center Across Selection from the *drop-down* list in the *Horizontal* section (figure 8.8).
9. **Click** OK.
10. **Select** noncontiguous range of cells: D6 through D22, B9 and C9, B20 and C20, and B22 and C22 as in figure 8.9. (Use the control

	A	B	C	D
1	MODERN SCHOOL OF VIRGINIA			
2	CHRISTMAS PARTY			
3	12/20/02			
4				
5	**DONATIONS AND COLLECTIONS**	9th Graders	10th Graders	Totals
6	Parents' Donations			
7	Students' Collections			
8				
9	Total Donations and Collections			
10				
11	**EXPENSE TYPES**			
12	Drinks			
13	Music			
14	Disposable plates, glasses, etc.			
15	Cleaning			
16	Guard Service			
17	Food			
18	Miscellaneous			
19				
20	Total Expenses			
21				
22	**Total Request from School**			
23				

Figure 8.6.   Budget Planning Spreadsheet with Labels and Numbers

key to select noncontiguous range. If this fails, do the formatting one contiguous range at a time.)

11. **Click** Format in the *Menu* bar and then on Cells . . . in the *Format* menu. The system displays figure 8.10 for Format Cells window.
12. **Click** tab for Number in the *Format Cells* window.
13. **Make selections** of: Currency from the *Category* section, Dollar ($) from the *Symbol* section, and two (2) from the *Decimal places* section.
14. **Click** OK.
15. **Select** the noncontiguous cells B6 to C7 and B12 to C18. The selection is shown in figure 8.11.
16. **Click** Format in the *Menu* bar and then on Cells . . . in the *Format* menu. The system displays figure 8.12 for Format Cells window.
17. **Click** tab for Number.
18. **Make selections** of Number from the *Category* section, two (2) from the *Decimal places* section, and then check the box for Use 1000 Separator.

	A	B	C	D
1	MODERN SCHOOL OF VIRGINIA			
2	CHRISTMAS PARTY			
3	12/20/02			
4				
5	DONATIONS AND COLLECTIONS	9th Graders	10th Graders	Totals
6	Parents' Donations	500	1000	
7	Students' Collections	2000	2500	
8				
9	Total Donations and Collections			
10				
11	EXPENSE TYPES			
12	Drinks	500	600	
13	Music	400	400	
14	Disposable plates, glasses, etc.	250	300	
15	Cleaning	120	125	
16	Guard Service	150	150	
17	Food	2200	2210	
18	Miscellaneous	200	250	
19				
20	Total Expenses			
21				
22	Total Request from School			
23				

Figure 8.7. Data Entry in a Spreadsheet

19. **Click** <u>OK</u>. The complete Excel budget spreadsheet with all of the formatting changes is shown in figure 8.13.
20. **Click** the <u>Save</u> icon on the *Standard* toolbar to save the changes.

ONE-YEAR ELECTRONIC GRADE BOOK

Let's assume you are a math teacher who was teaching Introduction to Basic Algebra as one of the courses during the fall semester 2002. You will assign final grades to students based on the accumulated performance on three tests, a final examination, and some bonus points earned throughout the term. The grading formula is strictly based on the time-honored grading scheme of $90-100 = A$; $80-89 = B$; $70-79 = C$; $60-69 = D$; $0-59 = F$. Each test and the final exam is worth a maximum of 100 points each, and a

Dialogue 8.2.   A Dialogue Session for Using Functions and Formulas in an Excel Spreadsheet

Below is an excerpt from an actual computer training session

Session Dialogue		Teaching Principles (*) Management Tactics (■) Illustrated
Teacher	First, **click** in cell D6. Now, **click** on the AutoSum icon in the *Standard toolbar*, and then **press** the <Enter> key. What did you get, Claudia?	
Claudia	I got an answer of 1500. Can I format this number to put in a dollar sign?	
Teacher	You are way ahead of me, but that is very good. We'll come back to that later. What does 1500 represent in cell D6, Dawn?	
Dawn	The sum of two cells B6 containing 500 and C6 with 1000.	* * ■ * ■
Teacher	I like it. How can we get similar results for cell D7, Jo?	
Jo	First, **click** in cell D7. Then, **click** on the AutoSum icon in the *Standard toolbar*, and then **press** the <Enter> key.	
Teacher	Excellent answer. Now, what about getting similar answers for B9, C9, and D9, Dorothy?	
Dorothy	Same as before: First, **click** in cell B9. Then, **click** on the AutoSum icon in the *Standard toolbar,* and then **press** the <Enter> key.	
Georges	First, **click** in cell C9. Then, **click** on the AutoSum icon in the *Standard toolbar*, and then **press** the <Enter> key.	
Julius	Same as before: First, **click** in cell D9. Then, **click** on the AutoSum icon in the *Standard toolbar,* and then **press** the <Enter> key. The system displays the answers.	

The vertical column heads read, left to right: Students learn new concepts hands-on; Students participated in their learning; Call students by name; Use inductive approach; Gain and maintain attention.

	A	B	C	D
1	MODERN SCHOOL OF VIRGINIA			
2	CHRISTMAS PARTY			
3	12/20/02			
4				
5	DONATIONS AND COLLECTIONS	9th Graders	10th Graders	Totals
6	Parents' Donations	500	1000	1500
7	Students' Collections	2000	2500	4500
8				
9	Total Donations and Collections	2500	3500	6000

Matthew	Can we do this any faster?	
Teacher	We will try. There is no harm in trying.	

Students	OK.
Teacher	**Click** in cell D12. Now **click** on the Au-toSum icon in the *Standard toolbar*, and then **press** the <Enter> key. Did you get an answer of 1100, Ogechi?
Ogechi	Yes. Now, can we do it any faster?
Teacher	Let us try. **Click** back in cell D12. **Position** the mouse pointer in the copying position. **Click** and **drag** to cell D18. Look for the answers that are shown.

	A	B	C	D
1	MODERN SCHOOL OF VIRGINIA			
2	CHRISTMAS PARTY			
3	12/20/02			
4				
5	DONATIONS AND COLLECTIONS	9th Graders	10th Graders	Totals
6	Parents' Donations	500	1000	1500
7	Students' Collections	2000	2500	4500
8				
9	Total Donations and Collections	2500	3500	6000
10				
11	EXPENSE TYPES			
12	Drinks	500	600	1100
13	Music	400	400	800
14	Disposable plates, glasses, etc.	250	300	550
15	Cleaning	120	125	245
16	Guard Service	150	150	300
17	Food	2200	2210	4410
18	Miscellaneous	200	250	450
19				

Nike	Can we try something else?
Teacher	Absolutely.
Shanette	Everyone **click** in cell B20. Now **click** on the AutoSum icon in the *Standard toolbar*, and then **press** the <Enter> key. Did everybody get an answer of 3820?
Students	Yes.
Sibel	Now, **Click** back in cell B20. **Position** the mouse pointer in the copying position. **Click** and **drag** to cell D20. (*Look for the answers that are shown towards the end of this dialogue.*)
Teacher	Wonderful. One more thing before we finish this and take a short break. Can we now calculate the amount to be requested from school officials?
Tameka	That is easy. Just subtract donations from expenses.
Teacher	Let us **click** in cell B22. Can you give me the formula for this, Ihuoma?
Ihuoma	**Type** the required equal (=) sign and then **type** B9-B20.
Teacher	Students, do you agree?
Students	(*Complete silence for few seconds.*) It is not correct. It should be the other way around.

Example of a "Good error"

(continues)

Dialogue 8.2.   (Continued)

Below is an excerpt from an actual computer training session

Session Dialogue		Teaching Principles (*) Management Tactics (■) Illustrated
Teacher	You mean, = B20-B9	
Carolyn	Yes, but it was tricky.	
Teacher	Agree. Now, everyone **type** this formula in cell B22 and **press** the <Enter> key. Did you get an answer of 1320?	
Students	Yes.	
Teacher	Are we finished?	
Students	Not yet. We need to copy the formula from B22 to C22 and D22.	
Teacher	How do we do that, Ann?	
Ann	**Click**, everybody, back in cell **B22**. **Position** the mouse pointer in the copying position. **Click** and **drag** to cell D22. The answers are shown.	

	A	B	C	D
1	MODERN SCHOOL OF VIRGINIA			
2	CHRISTMAS PARTY			
3	12/20/02			
4				
5	DONATIONS AND COLLECTIONS	9th Graders	10th Graders	Totals
6	Parents' Donations	500	1000	1500
7	Students' Collections	2000	2500	4500
8				
9	Total Donations and Collections	2500	3500	6000
10				
11	EXPENSE TYPES			
12	Drinks	500	600	1100
13	Music	400	400	800
14	Disposable plates, glasses, etc.	250	300	550
15	Cleaning	120	125	245
16	Guard Service	150	150	300
17	Food	2200	2210	4410
18	Miscellaneous	200	250	450
19				
20	Total Expenses	3820	4035	7855
21				
22	Total Request from School	1320	535	1855
23				

student can earn a maximum of 10 bonus points. The average for each test and the bonus points are also computed. All you as an individual or a trainer have to do is to first open the template and then type scores for each student. Only the first names of students are shown here because of privacy concerns. As the teacher, you could include the Social Security number and e-mail address for each student for easy referencing.

Opening the Template

1. **Click** the Open icon in the *Standard* toolbar. The Open dialog window opens (figure 8.14).

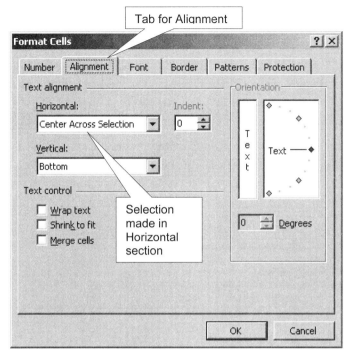

Figure 8.8. Centering Text in Multiple Rows Cells across Columns

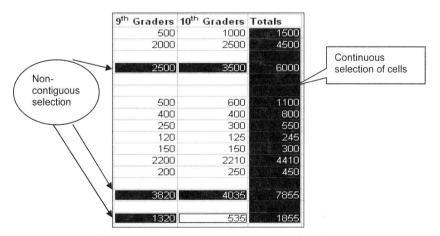

Figure 8.9. Contiguous and Noncontiguous Selection of Cells

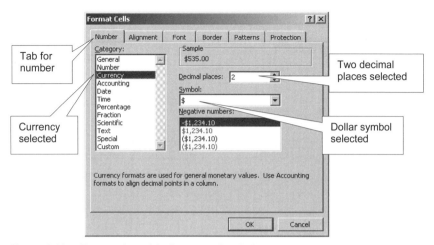

Tab for number

Currency selected

Two decimal places selected

Dollar symbol selected

Figure 8.10.   Formatting with Currency Symbol

9ᵗʰ Graders	10ᵗʰ Graders	Totals
500	1000	$1,500.00
2000	2500	$4,500.00
$2,500.00	$3,500.00	$6,000.00
500	600	$1,100.00
400	400	$800.00
250	300	$550.00
120	125	$245.00
150	150	$300.00
2200	2210	$4,410.00
200	250	$450.00
$3,820.00	$4,035.00	$7,855.00
$1,320.00	$535.00	$1,855.00

Figure 8.11.   Noncontiguous Selection of Cells for Formatting

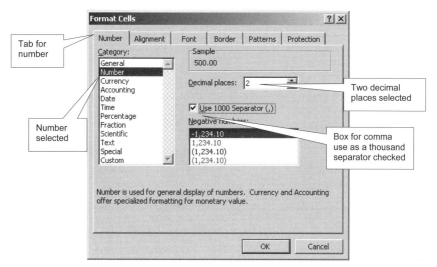

Figure 8.12.   Formatting with Currency Symbol

2. **Select** Chapter8 folder in the *Look In* box from the list in the drop-down arrow. You might have to double-click on the C: drive first and then on the Chapter8 folder to open it.
3. **Select** One-year Grade Book from the list of files. This file will serve as the template (figure 8.14).
4. **Click** Open to open the Excel file. The template is shown in figure 8.15.

Sometimes, the file extension (.XLS) is shown, but other times it is not. You should not be concerned with this minor detail because it depends on the set-up of the Windows operating system.

Entering Information in the Template

1. **Type** student test scores and bonus points as shown in figure 8.16. The grades, the average for each test, the final exam, and the bonus points are automatically computed based on a formula that is embedded in cells. The information is entered for each test as it occurs throughout the whole semester.
2. **Save** the changes.

	A	B	C	D
1	MODERN SCHOOL OF VIRGINIA			
2	CHRISTMAS PARTY			
3	12/20/02			
4				
5	DONATIONS AND COLLECTIONS	9th Graders	10th Graders	Totals
6	Parents' Donations	500.00	1,000.00	$1,500.00
7	Students' Collections	2,000.00	2,500.00	$4,500.00
8				
9	Total Donations and Collections	$2,500.00	$3,500.00	$6,000.00
10				
11	EXPENSE TYPES			
12	Drinks	500.00	600.00	$1,100.00
13	Music	400.00	400.00	$800.00
14	Disposable plates, glasses, etc.	250.00	300.00	$550.00
15	Cleaning	120.00	125.00	$245.00
16	Guard Service	150.00	150.00	$300.00
17	Food	2,200.00	2,210.00	$4,410.00
18	Miscellaneous	200.00	250.00	$450.00
19				
20	Total Expenses	$3,820.00	$4,035.00	$7,855.00
21				
22	Total Request from School	$1,320.00	$535.00	$1,855.00
23				

Figure 8.13.   The Budget Request Spreadsheet with All Format Changes

For multiple courses during the same term, **select** all applicable cells (in this case, A1 to H19), copy the selected range to the clipboard, and then paste the range in a different location. (Hint: first, **click** on the Copy icon in the *Standard* toolbar; second, **click** in cell A25; and finally **click** on the Paste icon in the *Standard* toolbar.) You can then change the name of the students, the course name, and the term name that are appropriate for the course. This pattern can then be repeated for a series of courses.

MULTIYEAR ELECTRONIC GRADE BOOK

This section is a continuation of the previous one. In this case, you as the math teacher want to create a similar grade book for academic year 2003 without spending an inordinate amount of time.

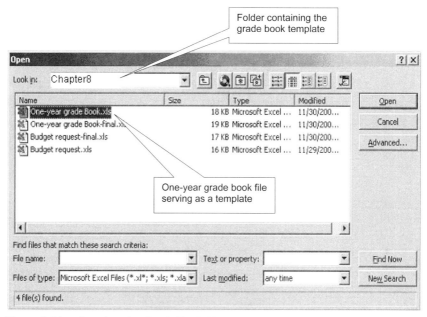

Folder containing the grade book template

One-year grade book file serving as a template

Figure 8.14. Opening the Grade Book Template

	A	B	C	D	E	F	G	H
1	INTRODUCTION TO COLLEGE PHYSICS							
2	Fall 2002							
3								
4		SCORES/GRADES						
5	Student Name	Test 1	Test 2	Test 3	Final	Bonus Points	Total Points	Final Grade
6								
7	Amie						0	
8	Barbara						0	
9	Becky						0	
10	Bob						0	
11	Eric						0	
12	Gabriel						0	
13	Jackie						0	
14	John						0	
15	Julie						0	
16	Mac						0	
17								
18	Average	0	0	0	0	0	0	
19								

Figure 8.15. One-Year Grade Book Template

	A	B	C	D	E	F	G	H
1	INTRODUCTION TO BASIC ALGEBRA							
2	Fall 2002							
3								
4		SCORES/GRADES						
5	Student Name	Test 1	Test 2	Test 3	Final	Bonus Points	Total Points	Final Grade
6								
7	Amie	80	82	91	81	2	336	B
8	Barbara	91	94	98	94	0	377	A
9	Becky	95	84	95	90	4	368	A
10	Bob	99	89	98	100	0	386	A
11	Eric	100	100	97	94	0	391	A
12	Gabriel	77	83	82	71	7	320	B
13	Jackie	68	71	65	68	8	280	C
14	John	55	51	71	45	3	225	F
15	Julie	88	91	99	91	3	372	A
16	Mac	86	92	92	88	6	364	A
17								
18	Average	83.9	83.7	88.8	82.2	3.3	341.9	
19								

Figure 8.16. Test Scores for Each Test and Final Exam and Final Letter Grades in a Course

Highlighting the Whole Sheet

1. **Click** on <u>Select All Button</u> to select all cells in *Sheet1* of the book (figure 8.17).
2. **Click** the <u>Copy</u> icon on the *Standard* toolbar. This will copy the selected range to the clipboard.

Renaming a Sheet

1. **Click** <u>Sheet2</u> in the *Sheet tabs*.
2. **Right-click** the <u>tab</u> for *Sheet2*. The pop-up menu shown in figure 8.18 appears.

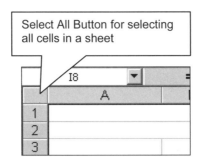

Figure 8.17. Select All Button for Selecting the Entire Sheet

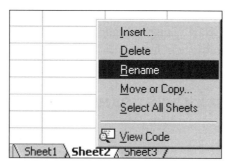

Figure 8.18. Renaming a Sheet

3. **Click** the Rename choice and **type** AY2003 on top of Sheet2 and **press** the <Enter> key. The new name appears instead of Sheet2 as shown in figure 8.19.

Pasting across Sheets

1. **Click** in Cell A1. Make sure that the AY2003 sheet is current.
2. **Click** the Paste icon in the *Standard* toolbar. This will paste the selected range from the clipboard to this sheet.
3. **Press** <Ctrl-Home> to deselect the range and move to cell A1.
4. Save this Excel book under a different name (e.g., Multiyear Grade Book) in the Chapter8 folder. (Hint: **Click** File/Save as . . . to start saving it under a different name.)
5. **Change** Fall 2002 to Fall 2003 in cell A2, and change Algebra to Math in cell A1.
6. **Change** student names to reflect the names of students enrolled in

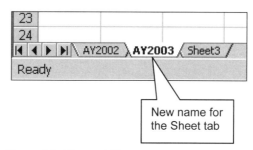

New name for the Sheet tab

Figure 8.19. A Sheet with Changed Name

the fall term of 2003 and also the grades for Test1 and Test2 to see the impact of these changes on the final grade. The Excel book with the changes is shown in figure 8.20.

SEARCHING FOR STUDENT NAMES IN AN EXCEL BOOK

1. **Click** in the tab for *AY2002* sheet.
2. **Press** the Shift key and keep it pressed and then **click** on the tab for *AY2003*. This will select tabs for both sheets. This technique allows you to make a contiguous selection of sheets.
3. **Click** Edit in the *Menu* bar. Figure 8.21 will be displayed in response to this action.
4. **Click** Find in the *Edit* menu. Figure 8.22 for Find window is displayed.
5. **Type** "tracy" (type the text without quotation marks) in the *text box* for Find what:. The search is *not* case sensitive.
6. **Click** Find Next. The system will move to AY2003 sheet and move to the cell containing Tracy as a student name.

	A	B	C	D	E	F	G	H
1			INTRODUCTION TO BASIC MATH					
2			Fall 2003					
3								
4				SCORES/GRADES				
5	Student Name	Test 1	Test 2	Test 3	Final	Bonus Points	Total Points	Final Grade
6								
7	Andrea	90	90	91	81	2	354	B
8	Celestine	100	94	98	94	0	386	A
9	Chevelle	90	90	95	90	4	369	A
10	Kevin	100	91	98	100	0	389	A
11	Khadija	87	77	97	94	0	355	B
12	Omar	89	85	82	71	7	334	B
13	Pamela	98	75	65	68	8	314	C
14	Sharah	100	89	71	45	3	308	C
15	Tod	55	99	99	91	3	347	B
16	Tracy	76	100	92	88	6	362	A
17								
18	Average	88.5	89	88.8	82.2	3.3	351.8	
19								

Figure 8.20. Completed Multiyear Grade Book with Final Grades and Averages

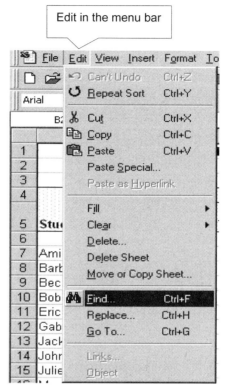

Figure 8.21.   Searching Information in an Excel Book

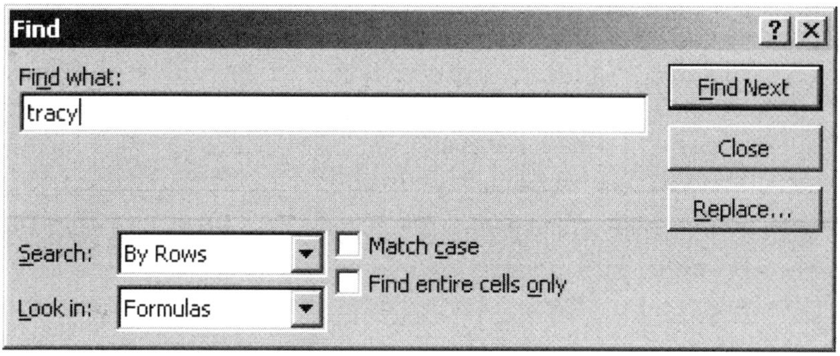

Figure 8.22.   The Final Dialog Window in Excel 97

7. **Click** Close.
8. **Click** the Save icon on the *Standard* toolbar to save the changes.

This type of recordkeeping will assist you in locating students who took your course a long time ago and are now looking for a letter of recommendation or reference. Also, it will assist you in answering questions if there is a challenge on a grade and in preparing reports requested by the administration.

Authors' Note: You must practice and practice to become comfortable in the use of applications that are described here. Also, you must spend time to learn the basic commands in a spreadsheet.

TRAINER DIRECTED/INDIVIDUAL READER EXERCISES

1. Examine the formulas in calculated cells in the electronic grade book(s).
2. Type Student Name for Column heading in cell A4.
3. Enter names for ten students in cells A5 to A14.
4. Type the names of three courses in cells B4 to D4.
5. Enter letter grades for all ten students in all three courses in cells B5 to D14.
6. Provide a Column heading GPA in cell E4.
7. Compute the Grade Point Average (GPA) for the first student in cell E5 based on academic standards. In your calculations, assume that the first course is two credit hours, second course is four credit hours, and the third course is three credit hours.
8. Copy the formula in cell E5 to E6 to E14.
9. Format cells to make your work attractive.

9

SHOWING OFF WITH POWERPOINT

You want to sparkle for your class? Dazzle your colleagues in professional meetings? We do. You can do it, too, when you are making a presentation. A program such as Presentations or PowerPoint can help you do this. For this book, we have chosen PowerPoint because of its worldwide availability and its use. This program offers all the features that you are familiar with in using slides, transparencies, and overhead projectors. Essentially, Power-Point replaces all of the past devices people used in classroom presentations, at professional meetings, or during large gatherings. If you learn PowerPoint yourself, you can help your students dazzle their colleagues when making presentations themselves. And surprise, surprise! PowerPoint is relatively easy to learn and use. We are taking mercy on you for the time being.

BASICS OF POWERPOINT 97

In this chapter, you will create a PowerPoint presentation (slide show) using a template provided by the program.

Start PowerPoint 97

1. If the PowerPoint icon is already on your Desktop, **double-click** on it. The system will open the PowerPoint program and display the window shown in figure 9.1. Skip over steps 2, 3, and 4. Otherwise, proceed to step 2 and then continue.
2. **Click** Start on the extreme left of the *Taskbar*.
3. **Click** Programs on the *Start* menu.

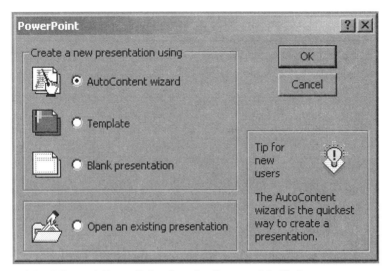

Figure 9.1.   Microsoft PowerPoint Opening Screen with Choices

4. **Click** <u>PowerPoint</u> in the list. These actions will open the PowerPoint window shown in figure 9.1.

You have four choices as indicated by the options buttons: AutoContent Wizard (the default choice), Template, Blank Presentation, and Open an Existing Presentation. First, we will open Template and explain the features of PowerPoint with its help. After this, you will be able to create for yourself a similar presentation in less than half an hour.

Before we discuss these features, it is essential that you familiarize yourself with various parts of the PowerPoint window described in figure 9.2.

Open a Template

A template, in general, resembles office stationery where some of the items are already printed. In PowerPoint, a template is a kind of complete slide show for a specific purpose. These templates are already installed as part of your PowerPoint program. We have opened one template to assist us in explaining the different icons on the PowerPoint Toolbars. Don't be clicking around . . . yet.

1. **Click** the choice for <u>Template,</u> and then **click** <u>OK</u>. The system will open a screen for a new presentation as shown in figure 9.3.

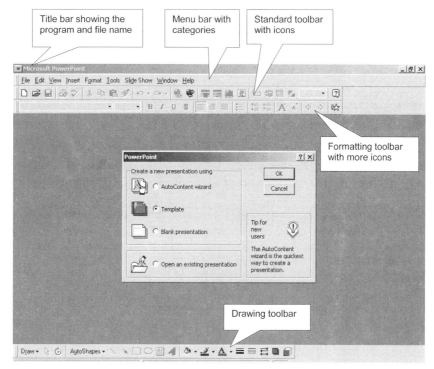

Figure 9.2.   PowerPoint Program Main Window with a New Presentation

2. **Click** the tab for Presentations.
3. **Click** the template for Project Overview (Standard). You might have to scroll down vertically to locate this template.
4. **Click** OK to complete this selection. The system displays the first slide of the template (figure 9.4).

Description of Toolbars

To display the meaning of any icon on the toolbars, all you have to do is point (not click) the mouse pointer on the icon. As soon as you do this, the system displays the description of the icon. Figures 9.5 and 9.6 show the icons for the Standard toolbar and the Drawing toolbar.

1. **Click** Outline View (shown in figure 9.7) located near the *bottom left* of the slide. The Scroll bar for slides is shown in figure 9.8. The system displays text for the different slides of the template in the outline view as shown in figure 9.9.

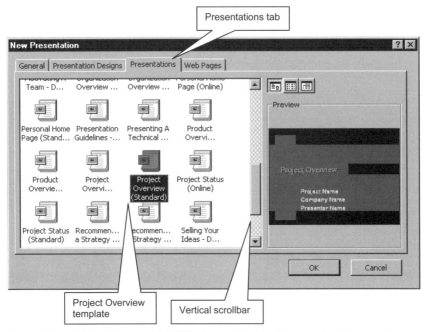

Figure 9.3.   A New Presentation Window with Templates under Presentations

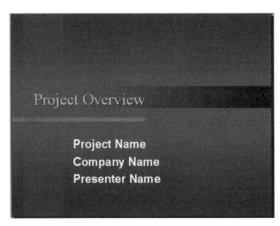

Figure 9.4.   First Slide of the Template

Figure 9.5. Description of Frequently Used Icons in Standard Toolbar

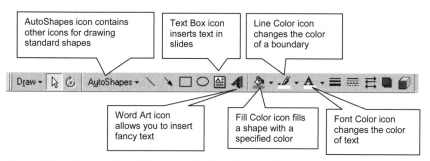

Figure 9.6. Description of Frequently Used Icons in Drawing Toolbar

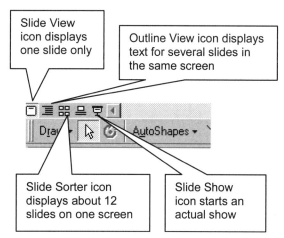

Figure 9.7. Description of Selected View Buttons

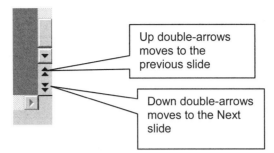

Figure 9.8. Slide Scroll Arrows Located toward the Bottom Right Corner of the Window

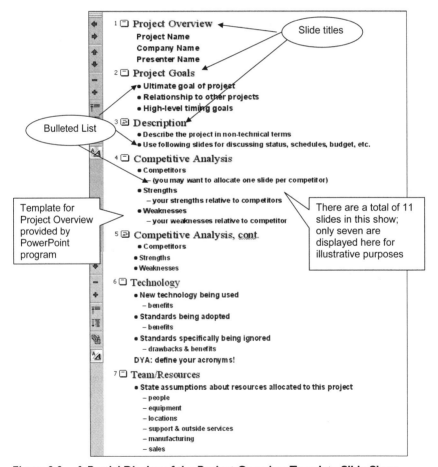

Figure 9.9. A Partial Display of the Project Overview Template Slide Show

CREATE YOUR SLIDE SHOW FROM A TEMPLATE

A template for a slide show is shown in the previous computer screen display (figure 9.9). As noted above, there are actually eleven slides, but only seven are shown here to illustrate the process. Your task is to replace the text of the template with the new text shown below. For example, the title of the first slide will be replaced with *The New American Teacher—Me*. The project name will be replaced by *An Experience-based Paradigm for Alternative Teacher Training*. The company name will be replaced by your school name and the presenter name will be replaced by your name. In the second slide, the title, Project Goals, will be replaced by *Chapter 1 title*. A complete display for the eleven new slides is shown below in figures 9.10A and 9.10B for the ease of inputting into the system. You will actually type this text.

Insert a Blank Slide

Having successfully completed eleven slides, you need to tell the world how wonderful you are on an additional slide, number 12. The title of the

Figure 9.10a. Text for Slides 1–6

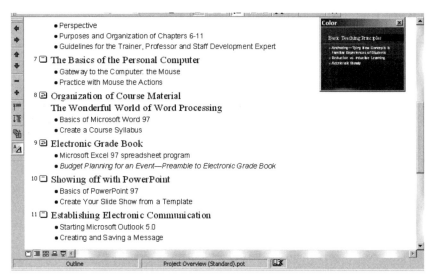

Figure 9.10b. Text for Slides 7–11

new slide will be Project Celebration with some ClipArt (graphic images provided by many computer programs) added to it. Now let's do it.

1. **Click** Slide View towards the *lower left corner of the slide window.*
2. **Press** <Ctrl-End> to move to the last slide in the show, in this case, slide 11.
3. **Click** the icon for New Slide in the *Standard toolbar* to insert a slide at the end of slide 11. In response to this command, the system displays a New Slide layout window as shown in figure 9.11.
4. **Click** the Title Only (*3rd row and 3rd column*) slide layout and then **click** OK. The system displays a blank slide as shown in figure 9.12.
5. **Click** in the text box Click to add title (figure 9.12).
6. **Input** the phrase Project Celebration.
7. **Click** *outside the text box* to view the text (figure 9.13).

Draw and Insert an AutoShape

Sometimes, you want to reflect a mood or a theme by including special graphics—but drawing these graphics can be very time-consuming and sometimes difficult. Nevertheless, they are useful and contribute to making

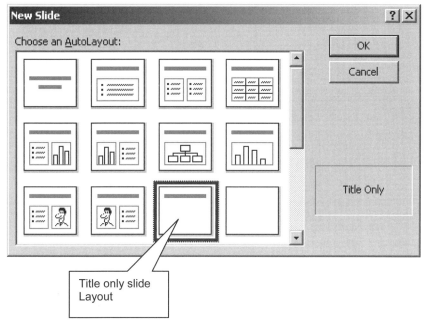

Figure 9.11.   New Slide AutoLayout Window

a presentation memorable. Cheers! You have a secret artist in your friend, the computer. The system makes it easy to be artistic by including many of these shapes under a category AutoShapes.

1. **Click** the AutoShapes icon in the *Drawing toolbar*. The system displays the categories of AutoShapes as shown in figure 9.14.
2. **Click** Stars and Banners.
3. **Click** the 5-Point Star (*1st row, 5th column*).
4. **Click** any starting point on the *slide* and then **<drag>** it to any other point on the slide using an approximately 45° angle. The result is shown in figure 9.15.

It is easy to make a mistake at first, but not to worry. If you make a mistake, **click** the object you drew and **press** the <Delete> key. Then start all over again. With some practice you will be able to draw this star and other figures as well.

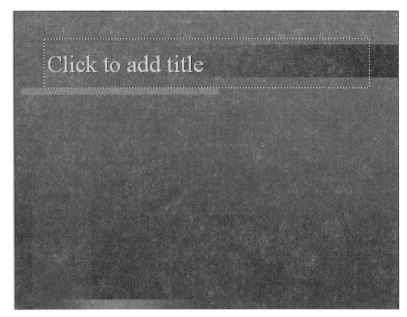

Figure 9.12. A Blank Title Slide Ready to Be Modified

Insert Clip Art

After looking at your star, maybe you speculate, "Well, I think I need something else to make this slide sparkle and fizz." We say, "Great thinking! How about some Clip Art to spice it up? Here's how to do it."

1. **Click** the Insert Clip Art icon in the *Standard toolbar*.
2. **Click** Entertainment category.
3. **Click** Entertainment, Victory bottle icon, and then **click** OK. The system inserts a champagne bottle in the slide as shown in figure 9.16.
4. **Resize** the champagne bottle to approximately 1.5" by 1.5". Use the handle to resize the bottle; it must be selected first.
5. **Click and drag** the bottle to the right-hand bottom corner of the slide away from the star as shown in figure 9.16.

Change Fill Color of the Star

Now that you've gotten the hang of these features, why not keep on going? Don't stop here!

Figure 9.13. A New Slide with the Title Project Celebration

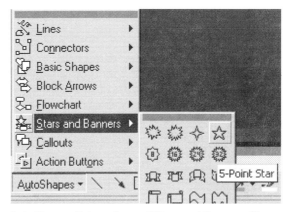

Figure 9.14. AutoShapes Categories and Stars and Banners Shapes

Figure 9.15.   A Slide with an AutoShape of a Star

1. **Select** the star by clicking in it. The system confirms the selection by placing handles around it.
2. **Click** the down-arrow for Fill Color icon in the *Drawing toolbar*. The result is shown in figure 9.17.
3. **Click** the More Fill Colors . . . choice.
4. **Click** the color of your choice (Blue) in the *Colors window*, and then **click** OK to confirm this selection. The star is now filled with blue color (dialogue 9.1). Now let's see if you can do all this fancy stuff.

Inserting a New Slide and Word Art

Dialogue 9.1 will reinforce your learning in this chapter. We want to insert a new slide in front (in position 12) of the last slide in the current set. As a result of this action, the current slide 12 will become slide 13. In the new slide, the title should be Project Summary, and we need to insert a WordArt phrase that states Award Winning Project of 2002 in the middle of the slide.

Figure 9.16.   A Slide with an AutoShape (Star) and Clip Art (Bottle)

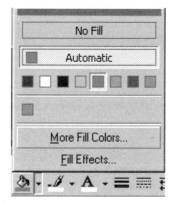

Figure 9.17.   Fill Color Selection

Dialogue 9.1.   A Sample Dialogue Session for Inserting a New Slide and WordArt

Below is an excerpt from an actual computer training session

Session Dialogue		Teaching Principles (*) Management Tactics (■) Illustrated
Teacher	We just inserted a new slide at the end of the template set. Now, we want to insert one more new slide just before the last slide. Where do you start, Elom?	
Elom	**Click** the <u>Slide View</u> button toward the lower left corner of the *slide window*.	
Teacher	That is good. What do we do next, Francisco?	* ■ * ■
Francisco	**Press** <Ctrl-End> to move to the last slide in the show.	Practice with learned concepts / Call students by name / Use inductive approach / Gain and maintain attention
Teacher	Is that the place we should be before we insert a new slide, Genet?	
Genet	No. We must move to the previous slide by clicking on the Previous Slide arrows toward the bottom of the vertical bar.	
Teacher	We are getting there. What is the next step, Glynis?	
Glynis	**Click** the icon for <u>New Slide</u> in the *Standard toolbar* and then **click** the <u>Title Only</u> (3rd row and 3rd slide layout) slide layout. Finally, **click** OK to complete the insertion.	
Teacher	Now, having inserted a blank slide, where do we type the title of the slide, Joanna?	
Joanna	**Click** in the text box for <u>Click to Add Title</u>, **type** Project Summary and then **click** outside the text box.	
Teacher	Wonderful. Last thing we have to do is to add WordArt in the slide. How do we proceed with this, Jose?	
Jose	**Click** on the <u>Insert WordArt</u> icon in the *Drawing toolbar*.	
	Click on one of the choices (3rd row and 2nd column) in the window for *WordArt Gallery*.	

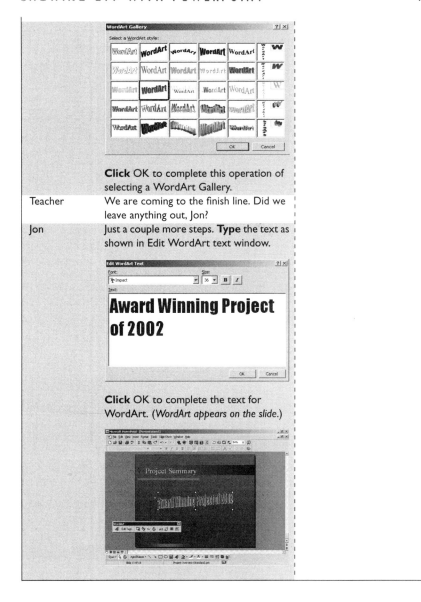

Click OK to complete this operation of selecting a WordArt Gallery.

Teacher   We are coming to the finish line. Did we leave anything out, Jon?

Jon   Just a couple more steps. Type the text as shown in Edit WordArt text window.

Click OK to complete the text for WordArt. (WordArt appears on the slide.)

The slide show for your project consisting of thirteen slides is now complete. Nifty?

Yes! Yes! Yes! Now you can take another break, and go have your own celebration.

RUN THE SLIDE SHOW

Now, it's show time.

1. **Press** <Ctrl-Home> to return to the first slide.
2. **Click** the icon for Slide Show in the *View Buttons* toward the lower left of the PowerPoint window.
3. Use the **left-click** of the mouse or the <**right-arrow**> key on the keyboard to forward a slide.
4. Use the **left-arrow** key on the keyboard to back up to the previous slide.
5. Use the <**Esc**> key anytime to terminate the slide show.

TRAINER DIRECTED/INDIVIDUAL READER EXERCISES

1. Create a folder, Chapter9, on the C: drive.
2. Open a template, "Thanking a Speaker . . ." from the tab group labeled Presentations.
3. Change the company name, TIS, to your school name.
4. Review all slides in the show.
5. Insert a blank slide at the end.
6. Create a "thank you" message for the trainer in your training.
7. Save this file as *Thank you note-1* in Chapter9 folder.

⑩

ELECTRONIC COMMUNICATION

Why should you add e-mail to your teaching repertoire? Well, for openers, it's fast, it's effective, and the kids think it's cool. After all, you don't want to be viewed as a dinosaur. Simply put, it can eliminate your road rage with regard to broken-down copying or fax machines, the time and tedium of writing an assignment on the chalkboard, or placing endless and time-consuming individual phone calls to students. Let us assure you we've had to cope with these happenings a whole lot. Finally, a breakthrough. You now can distribute assignments to students, inform students about changes in scheduling, and post grades on assignments and courses electronically. And you can do all these things for a group as a whole. On a more private basis, you can answer an individual student or parent inquiry without having to worry about calling someone at an inconvenient time. You also can send an assignment to or receive one from a student who has been unable to attend class.

An unexpected benefit for the students is they will find themselves having to write. Because they have to communicate, they may gradually feel more at ease in writing—and perhaps even improve their writing as well—through sheer practice. Are you now convinced of e-mail's benefits? We've been convinced for a long time.

In this chapter, we use Outlook Express 6.0 rather than Outlook to illustrate important tasks in electronic communication. Outlook Express is somewhat faster and easier to use than its more comprehensive version called Outlook.

STARTING MICROSOFT OUTLOOK EXPRESS 6.0

1. **Double-click** the Outlook Express icon on the *Desktop*. The system opens the Outlook Express program and displays figure 10.1 for the program.

Before you use this program, you need to be familiar with the various parts of the Outlook Express windows described in figure 10.2 and figure 10.3.

CREATE AND SAVE A MESSAGE

1. **Click** the New Mail icon in the *Toolbar*. The system displays the New Mail window, figure 10.4.
2. **Type** appropriate e-mail addresses in the To: and Cc: blocks and a subject heading in Subject: lines as shown in figure 10.4. In these pre-sentations, yyy is used as a placeholder for a person's e-mail address.
3. **Type** information in the message window with your name at the bottom. Your name at the bottom is treated as a signature in electronic communication.

Why is it that you can always count on being interrupted in the midst of preparing a message? Worse, you have to leave your computer right away. In such cases, save the message before you log off your computer. The message saved this way is stored in the Drafts folder.

1. **Click** File in the *Menu* bar.
2. **Click** Save on the *File* menu. This action saves the e-mail you are composing in the Drafts folder.

RETRIEVE SAVED E-MAIL FROM THE DRAFTS FOLDER

Once a message has been saved in the Drafts folder, you need to retrieve it before you can make changes to it or before you send it.

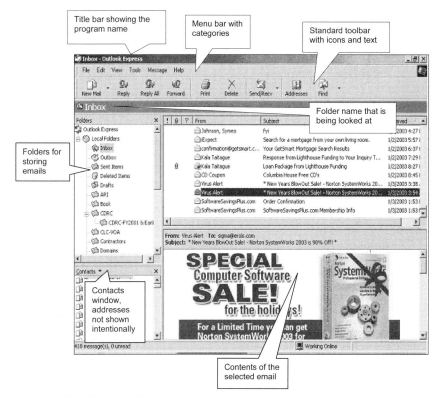

Figure 10.1. Microsoft Outlook Express Opening Screen

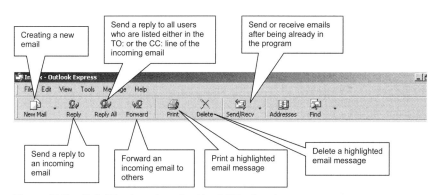

Figure 10.2. Brief Explanations for Useful Toolbar Icons

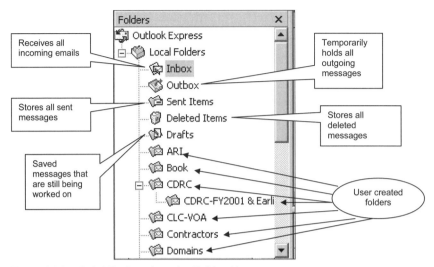

Figure 10.3.   Brief Explanations for Folder Names

1. **Click** Drafts folder in the *Folder* panel as shown in figure 10.5.
2. **Double-click** the message on the *right-hand* panel as shown above. This action will open the message window as shown in figure 10.6.
3. Make the necessary changes in the message window.

SEND A MESSAGE

1. **Click** Send in the *Toolbar*. The message will be sent to all users whose e-mail addresses are included in the To: and Cc: lines. If the e-mail address is wrong, the system will inform you the message could not be delivered to that individual or group of individuals.

SEND ASSIGNMENTS AS E-MAIL ATTACHMENTS

Tests, assignments, and other schoolwork that you have worked on in the computer are saved as computer files. When a computer file of some schoolwork or assignment is sent via e-mail, it is an e-mail attachment. You can send one or more e-mail attachments at a time. For this first exercise, we will create a short e-mail message and send an attachment from a folder

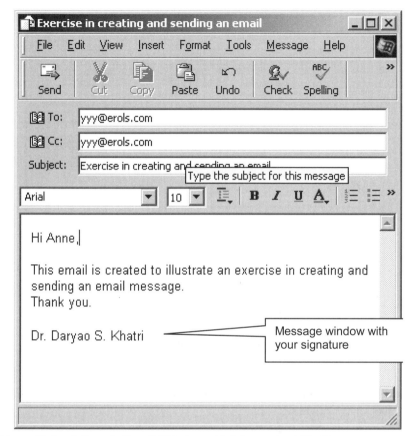

Figure 10.4.   A Sample E-mail Window with Information Filled In

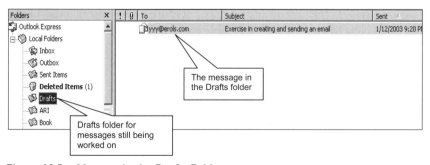

Figure 10.5.   Message in the Drafts Folder

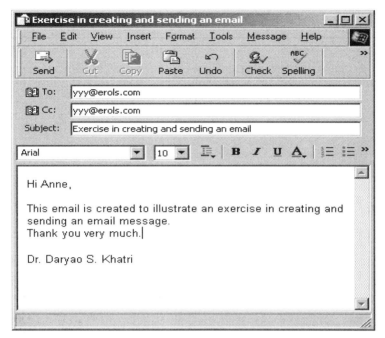

Figure 10.6. Message as Retrieved from the Drafts Folder

named Chapter7 on the C: drive. Later on, you can practice with folders and files of your own.

Here are the steps to do this task.

1. **Click** >> located to the *right side of the e-mail* window. The system displays the hidden icons of the Toolbar as shown and to the side in figure 10.7.

   Note: If the e-mail window for creating a message is maximized, the icon for Attach will be visible right there on the toolbar. In that case, you can click on Attach (or its icon shown by the paper clip).

2. **Click** Attach in the list. The system displays figure 10.8 for Insert Attachment.

3. **Select** appropriate folders and file(s). Choose noncontiguous files by using the <Ctrl> key in conjunction with the mouse click.

4. **Click** Attach to exit this window and move back to the mail Window. In response, the system displays figure 10.9 with the filenames shown in the Attach line.

Figure 10.7. Getting to the Attach Icon

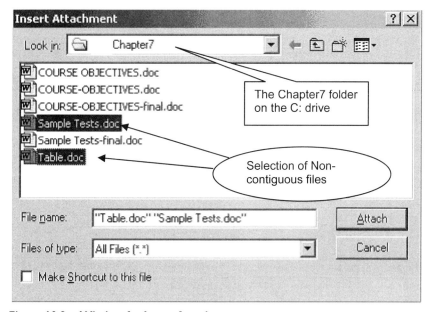

Figure 10.8. Window for Insert Attachment

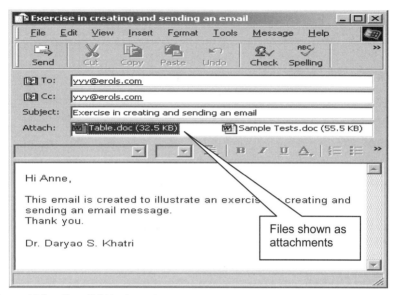

Figure 10.9. E-mail Attachments

5. Make necessary changes to the e-mail message. The e-mail window with the changes is shown in figure 10.10.
6. **Click** <u>Send</u> in the *Toolbar* when you are ready to send it.

The e-mail attachments will be sent to the user along with the message. In order to read the e-mail attachment, the user on the other end must have the same program (e.g., Word) in which the attachment was created. For example, if you are sending a spreadsheet prepared using Excel 2000 as an attachment to your friend, your friend also must have the Excel 2000 program (and not Excel 97) installed on his or her computer. Otherwise, the attachment can't be read.

E-MAIL DISTRIBUTION (GROUP) LIST

When you have a large number of students or colleagues to whom you send e-mails on a regular basis, sending them e-mails individually is very time consuming. A timesaving feature in e-mail for such a task is called a distribution (group) list.

This section has two parts. First, we will create a distribution list for all

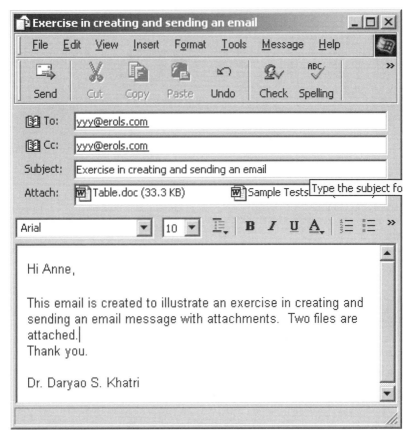

Figure 10.10. Changed E-mail Message Window after Its Initial Save in the Drafts Folder

teachers in the English department and label that list as TeachersEngDept. Second, we will create a distribution list for a class in prealgebra at the tenth-grade level and label this list as PreAlgebra10. The second list will be created with the help of students in a class and is shown in dialogue 10.1.

TeachersEngDept Distribution List

1. **Click** Addresses (Address Book) icon on the *Toolbar*. The system displays figure 10.11 for the Address Book.
2. **Click** File in the *Menu* bar. The system displays figure 10.12, the Address Book window.

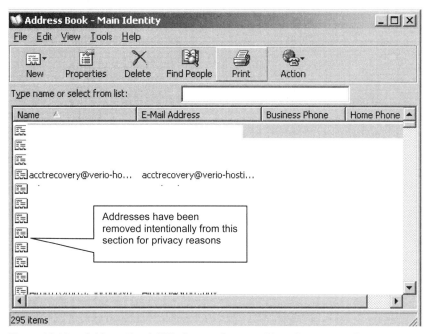

Figure 10.11. Address Book Window to Create a New Contact or Group List

3. **Click** New Group in the *File* menu.
   The system displays figure 10.13, Properties window, for the group list.

4. **Type** the name of the group (TeachersEngDept) in the text box for Group Name.

5. **Click** Select Members to include the individual e-mail addresses in the group. The system displays the window for Select Group members as shown in figure 10.14.
   Note: If you have new contacts that are not in the Address Book, you must click on New Contact and type all the related information about each contact.

6. **Double-click** on the e-mail addresses on the left-hand side under the Name section you want included in the group list. All the selected e-mail addresses will appear on the right-hand side of the window under the Members section. Fictitious names have been chosen here for privacy concerns. In your case, these names will be real. A sample list might appear, as shown in figure 10.14.

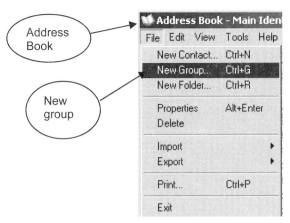

Figure 10.12. First Two Steps in Creating a Group List

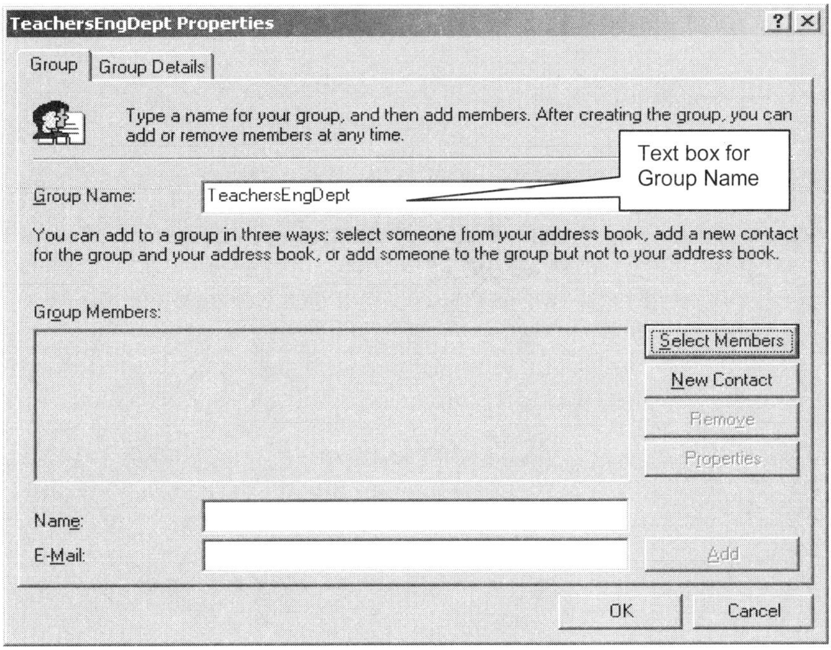

Figure 10.13. Properties Window for the Group List

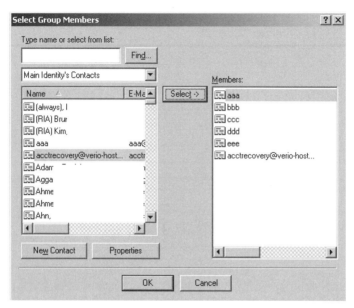

Figure 10.14. Select Group Members Window

7. **Click** OK located toward the bottom of the window after you have finished the selection. The system returns to the previous properties window as shown in figure 10.15.

8. **Click** OK in the window to finish this distribution list. The modified Address Book is shown in figure 10.16.

9. **Close** the window. The new distribution list is now available for use. It has been automatically saved. You use the distribution list in the same way you use a single person's e-mail address for sending e-mails.

PreAlgebra10 Distribution List

At this point, we are going to create another class distribution list for all students registered in a prealgebra course. The teacher uses this distribution list to communicate with students in this particular class. The distribution list is labeled as PreAlgebra10. Dialogue 10.1 is to show students' participation, test their understanding, and reinforce the commands learned by them.

The concept of creating a distribution list has been reinforced. In creating this distribution list, you, as a teacher, may have to add students' e-mail addresses in the Address Book first.

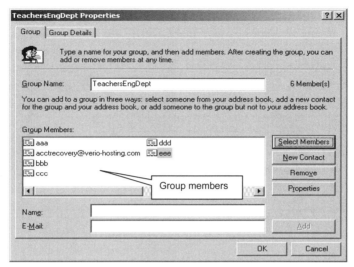

Figure 10.15. Group List Properties Window with Group Members Shown

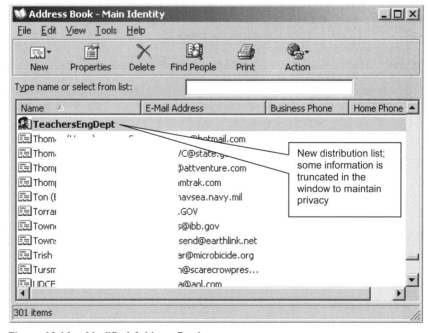

Figure 10.16. Modified Address Book

Dialogue 10.1. A Sample Dialogue Session for Creating an E-mail Group List

Below is an excerpt from an actual computer training session

Session Dialogue		Teaching Principles (*) Management Tactics (■) Illustrated
Teacher	What is the first step in creating a group (distribution) list for this class, Hamid?	* * ■ * ■
Hamid	**Click** on Addresses in the *Toolbar*.	
Teacher	That is good. What do we do next, So-losky?	
Solosky	**Click** File in the *Menu bar* and then New Group . . . from the File menu.	
Teacher	Excellent. What else do we do, Harold?	
Harold	**Type** PreAlgebra10 in the *Name Group* text box.	
Teacher	That is just fantastic. Is there anything else we need to do, Lee?	
Lee	Of course. **Click** the button for Select Members.	
Teacher	Quite right. What do we do next, Yan?	
Yan	**Double-click** the names you want to include in the group list under the *Name* column. (*The names will also appear under the Members column.*)	
Teacher	This is just wonderful and I love the input. Are we finished, Cathy?	
Cathy	Not really. We need to **Click** OK twice and then **close** the window for the Address Book.	
Teacher	You are just great. We have just created our own distribution list.	

Columns under Teaching Principles/Management Tactics Illustrated (read vertically): Reinforcement of concepts learned earlier | Students participated in their learning | Call students by name | Use inductive approach | Gain and maintain attention

Note: A distribution list is used just like an individual e-mail address. This type of list, however, will show in bold in your Address Book rather than in the regular font.

TRAINER DIRECTED/INDIVIDUAL READER EXERCISES

1. Create a class distribution list with about ten e-mail addresses in it and call it Class.
2. Send an e-mail with two e-mail attachments to all class participants in this distribution list.

❶❶

SEARCHING THE ELECTRONIC UNIVERSE

Do you remember visiting a candy store as a child? Oh, the wonder of it! All the splendid goodies spread out before you. We do, and you probably do, too. Well, now there's a nonfattening adult alternative for you. It's called the electronic universe, *aka* the Internet or the World Wide Web (WWW). The goodies on it make the candy store look like small potatoes. Here the goodies are information on virtually everything.

You, as a teacher, have an unparalleled opportunity to harness the excitement—and the goodies—of the Internet for both you and your students. And your students can do likewise.

In this chapter, we use Internet Explorer 6.0 as the browser to illustrate important tasks in information gathering on the Internet.

START INTERNET EXPLORER 6.0

1. **Double-click** the Internet Explorer icon on the *Desktop*. The system opens the Internet Explorer program and displays the following window for it, figure 11.1. The system opens an Internet site that has a URL (Uniform Resource Locator, the web address) set to the default setting. In this case, it opens the Yahoo website.

Before we discuss accessing a particular website, it is essential that you familiarize yourself with various parts of the Internet Explorer's Toolbar as described in figure 11.2.

Note: The text meaning of any icon can be displayed by pointing (not clicking) the mouse pointer to that icon.

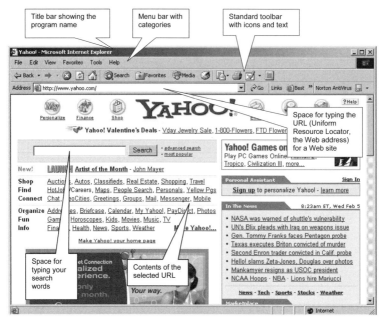

Title bar showing the program name

Menu bar with categories

Standard toolbar with icons and text

Space for typing the URL (Uniform Resource Locator, the Web address) for a Web site

Space for typing your search words

Contents of the selected URL

Figure 11.1.   Internet Explorer Opening Screen

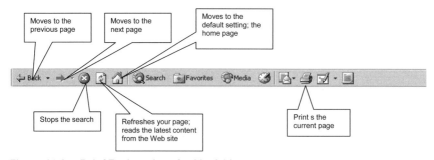

Moves to the previous page

Moves to the next page

Moves to the default setting; the home page

Stops the search

Refreshes your page; reads the latest content from the Web site

Print s the current page

Figure 11.2.   Brief Explanations for Useful Icons on the Toolbar

SEARCH TOOLS OF THE INTERNET

Before you can find information on the web, you need access to a search engine; it is also known by the names of *search site*, *search page*, or *search service*. Search sites or search engines have been set up by a variety of companies that offer you free web searching. Some common search engines are Yahoo, Excite, Alta Vista, Google, and Lycos. When you type the URL (Uniform Resource Locator) for these search engines, a web page is displayed where you can conduct your search.

Search engines are databases that store massive amounts of information gathered from millions of web pages. In spite of their sizes, however, they are relatively fast and are a quick way of locating information on the web. For the searches that follow, we will use either the Yahoo or the Google sites for searching information on the web.

FIND A URL FOR AN ORGANIZATION

A website's URL address can take many forms, but most of the largest ones have some uniformity in their URL. Sometimes, you can guess the address of these sites. For example, the URL for the Yahoo website is http://www.yahoo.com (http means Hypertext Transfer Protocol and is needed to satisfy the computer appetite). On the other hand, the URL for the U.S. Department of Transportation is http://www.dot.gov and for the White House it is http://www.whitehouse.gov. A difficulty is encountered if you have to guess the URL for the U.S. Department of Education or the U.S. Department of Energy. For a first guess, it could be http://www.doe.gov, but you can't be sure of it. To make certain of a URL for a website, there is a better way instead of wasting your time on continued guessing. The feature is called Autosearch.

All you have to do is delete what is already there in the URL line and type the name of the organization for which you are trying to find a URL. In the example that follows, we will try to find the URL of three organizations: the U.S. Department of Education, the U.S. Department of Energy, and the University of Delhi.

Find the URL for the Department of Education

1. **Select** the current URL address in the *Address* Line.
2. **Press** the <Delete> key on the keyboard.
3. **Type** the name of the organization (e.g., U.S. Department of Education) as shown in figure 11.3. The system displays the featured sites in figure 11.3.
4. **Press** the <Enter> key to complete the name of the organization.

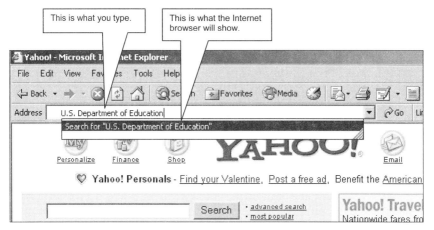

Figure 11.3.   Finding the URL for the U.S. Department of Education

The system displays figure 11.4 containing the URL for the Department of Education (only a portion of the screen is printed here).

Find the URL for the U.S. Department of Energy

1. **Select** the current URL address in the *Address* line.
2. **Press** the <Delete> key on the keyboard.

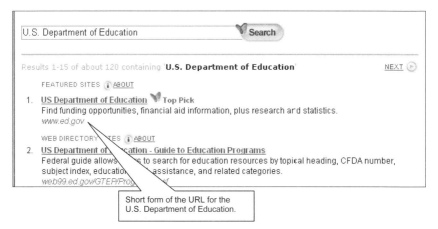

Figure 11.4.   Short Form of URL www.ed.gov for the U.S. Department of Education

3. **Type** the name of the organization (e.g., U.S. Department of Energy). When you are typing the name, the system will display the screen, figure 11.5.

4. **Press** the <Enter> key to complete the name of the organization. The system displays figure 11.6, containing the URL for the U.S. Department of Energy (only a portion of the screen is printed here).

Find the URL for the University of Delhi

1. **Select** the current URL address in the address line.
2. **Press** the <Delete> key on the keyboard.

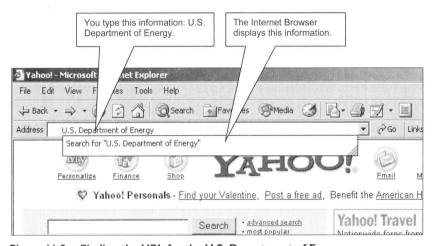

Figure 11.5. Finding the URL for the U.S. Department of Energy

Figure 11.6. Short Form of URL www.doe.gov for the U.S. Department of Energy

3. **Type** the name of the organization (e.g., University of Delhi). When you are typing the name, the system will display figure 11.7.
4. **Press** the <u><Enter></u> key to complete the name of the organization. The system displays figure 11.8 containing the URL for the University of Delhi (only a portion of the screen is printed here).

FIND A PERSON ON THE WEB

Not only can you search for organizations and institutions on the web but you can also search for people through either the Yahoo or Google search

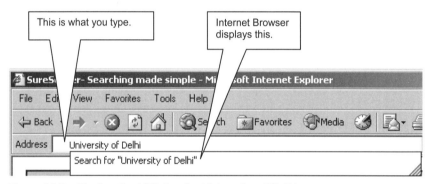

Figure 11.7.   Finding the URL for the University of Delhi

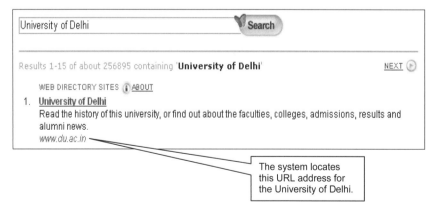

Figure 11.8.   Short Form of URL www.du.ac.in for the University of Delhi

engines. However, a search site labeled People Search (http://people.ya-hoo.com) provides a more focused search for people. It can scan a collection of databases for matching names by state in the union.

1. To search for a person, **type** the URL http://people.yahoo.com in the *Address* line of the Internet Browser.
2. **Press** the <u>Enter</u> key to complete the instruction. The browser displays figure 11.9.
3. **Type** the information of the name you have in the *First* and *Last Name* fields.
4. **Click** <u>Search</u>. In this example, we did not type any name. The system will display information for names matching your entry.

Follow instruction on this search page for the Advanced People Searches and searches for the White Pages or e-mail addresses.

FIND A JOB ON THE WEB

The web has many resources for job seekers. One of the more popular ones is the CareerBuilder, a database of classified ads compiled from hundreds of newspapers, which are constantly updated.

Figure 11.9. Finding a Person on the Web

1. You can access the CareerBuilder website by typing the URL address http://www.careerbuilder.com in the browser's *Address* line.
2. **Press** the <Enter> key after typing the Web address. The browser will display figure 11.10.
3. Follow instructions on the screen.

FIND COMPUTER SOFTWARE ON THE WEB

You can use the web to locate and/or purchase computer software, and receive and install demo versions of many computer software programs. It can also be used to download (to copy to your computer) thousands of useful free computer programs to your computer. The URL for this website is http://www.download.com. When you type this web address and **press** the <Enter> key, the browser displays figure 11.11.

After obtaining this web page, follow instructions on the search page to accomplish tasks.

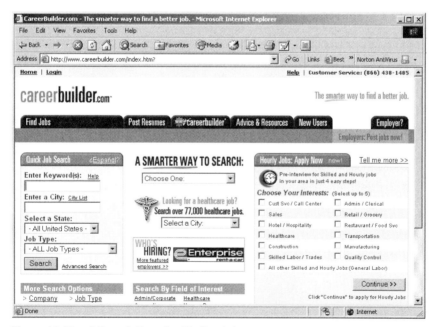

Figure 11.10. A Search Page for Finding Jobs

Figure 11.11.   A Screen Display of the Download Website

SEARCH THE WEB UNIVERSE

People search the web for many reasons. Teachers like to access information about topics they are either teaching or writing about. Graduating seniors in high school want to get information online about various colleges and universities. Some people just love to shop on the web. There is almost no limit to the kinds of tasks one can engage in when searching the web.

In this section, we take a very specific example to illustrate the use of the Google search engine. We use it first for a very broad search, and then use it to narrow the search. The exercise calls for finding the listings on the web for the authors' names (Daryao Khatri and Anne Hughes).

1. **Type** the URL address http://www.google.com in the URL address line as shown in figure 11.12.
2. **Press** the <Enter> key after typing this address. The browser will next display figure 11.13.
3. **Type** Khatri in the *search line* as the last name of the first author

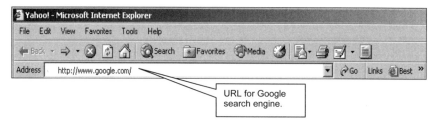

Figure 11.12.   Typing the URL for the Google Search Engine

Figure 11.13.   The First Screen for the Google Search Engine

and <**click**> on Google Search button. The system displays Figure 11.14. Since there are too many names, you need to narrow the search.

4. **Scroll** down the window and <**click**> on the hyperlink Search Within Results (figure 11.15).

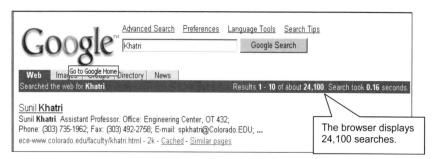

Figure 11.14.   The Search Engine Reports 24,100 Listings under Khatri

Figure 11.15.   The Option to Search within Results Displayed Previously

5. **Type** Hughes now in the search line for Search Within Results.
   Hughes is now added along with Khatri (figure 11.16).
6. **Click** the search button for Search Within Results. The browser now
   shows 596 entries when both names are used. Again, too many entries (figure 11.17).
7. **Scroll** down the window.
8. **Click** again on the hyperlink Search Within Results.
9. **Type** Daryao now in the search line for Search Within Results (figure 11.18).
10. **Click** the search button again for Search Within Results. The
    browser shows the results (figure 11.19) narrowed down to sixteen
    entries.

Let us reinforce the techniques you have learned using the search engines (dialogue 11.1).

Figure 11.16.   Narrowing Down Search to Khatri and Hughes

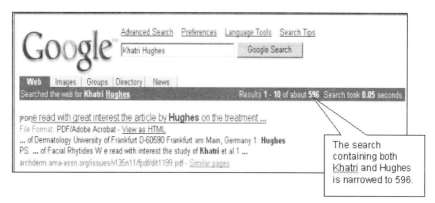

Figure 11.17.   The Search is Narrowed Down to 596 from an Initial High of 24,100

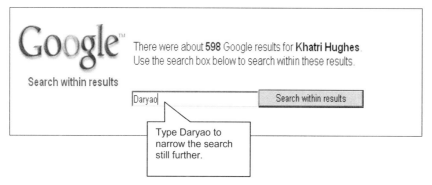

Figure 11.18.   Narrowing Down Search to Khatri, Hughes, and Daryao

Authors' note: Your search should take the pattern of an inverted pyramid. Start with one name first and gradually refine it, the model used in this case.

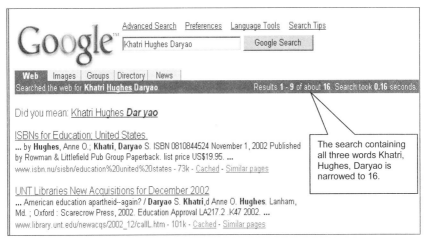

Figure 11.19. The Search Narrowed Down to 16

TRAINER DIRECTED/INDIVIDUAL READER EXERCISES

1. Find the URL for the University of California at San Diego.
2. Search the Internet for a book by Hilary Rodham Clinton, a U.S. senator from New York.

Dialogue 11.1.   A Sample Dialogue Session for Searching the Web

Below is an excerpt from an actual computer training session

Session Dialogue		Teaching Principles (*) Management Tactics (■) Illustrated
Teacher	Today, we want to search for a book titled Moby Dick by Herman Melville and edited by Harrison Hayford.	* * ■ * ■
Varney	That is easy. First, **type** the URL address http://www.google.com in the URL address line and **press** the <Enter> key.	Reinforcement of concepts learned earlier / Students participated in their learning / Call students by name / Use inductive approach / Gain and maintain attention
Tavare	Now, **type** Moby Dick in the search line and then **click** on the Google search button.	
Teacher	What did we get, Bill?	
Bill	Wow! We got 373,000 listings.	
Teacher	Quite right. And we would be wasting our time to try and look at such a monumental set of listings. What do we do next to narrow it down, Steve?	
Steve	**Scroll down** the search window and **click** on the Search Within Results hyperlink. Then, type Herman Melville in the search box.	
	Now, **click** the Search Within Results button to view the results of this search. In response, the browser displays the results of the search.	
Teacher	It is looking good, but still too many hits to be practical. What else can we do, Um?	

Um	One more thing. **Scroll down** the search window again and **click** on the Search Within Results hyperlink. Then, type Harrison Hayford in the search box.

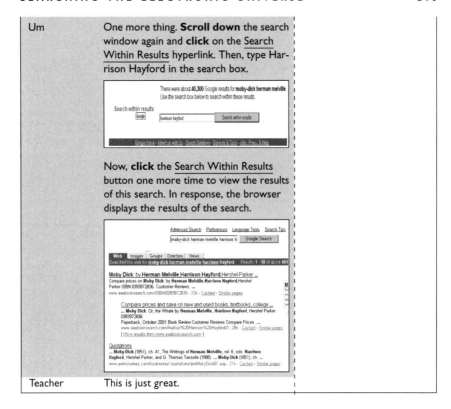

Now, **click** the Search Within Results button one more time to view the results of this search. In response, the browser displays the results of the search.

Teacher	This is just great.

Authors' Note: The steps for narrowing down an overly broad search have been reinforced because both teachers and students need to master these techniques in searching the web. Almost every search involves this process of narrowing down.

12

COMPLEX CONSTANTS OF TEACHING

Well now, we have pushed, pummeled, and propelled you through eleven chapters. Cheer up! There are only two more to go. And we are perfectly positive you will prevail. We shift from the variables of the teaching process, the pedagogical techniques, to something we have called the complex constants of the teaching process. We call them constants because they are present from the time you walk into your classroom until the time you leave it. In other words, they are always there in one form or another. We call them complex because they require your time, insight, patience, and knowledge. These constants are the diversity of your students; you, the teacher, as a participant-observer; the never-ending task of assessing students' learning; the use of technology; and the school and community resources available to you. These five constants are described and illustrated in this chapter.

DIVERSITY

Even when the students all look alike, come from the same social and economic backgrounds, and have the same culture, they are not alike. They may all look alike on the first day, but that's because you, the teacher, don't know them yet. As every teacher soon finds out—like about ten minutes into the first class period—each student is an individual with different talents, competencies, goals, anxieties, and dreams. But the teacher really discovers what individual differences are all about when the students come from different cultures, are only recent entrants into the American culture, speak languages other than English, are from very different social and economic backgrounds, and/or demonstrate an in-and-out attendance pattern throughout the semester. Variations on these kinds of individual differences currently are being played out in most of this nation's cities' public schools and close-in suburbs. And they have always been there in the rural backwaters and other remote communities. Whatever the particular variations of the differences are, they are likely to prove a challenge to whoever the teacher is, and you, as this teacher, will be expected to teach them all.

In an earlier book, we noted that the latest round of immigrants tended to cluster in certain urban areas and their inner rings of suburbs located on the east and west coasts based on the 2000 census.[1] This pattern is, if anything, intensifying as the nation deals with the aftermath of 9/11, the war in Iraq, and trouble in the Middle East and Africa. Newcomers, particularly if their political, cultural, and financial circumstances seem uncertain to them, huddle together for comfort's sake. Also, the springing up of local newspapers as well as radio and television stations in the languages of the newcomers are other efforts to have a sense of home and culture and to expand their "comfort" zones. For the parents and grandparents of these children, English-language learning may or may not be viewed as essential by them, although they will soon learn that virtually every job paying a living wage requires English. Inevitably, this resistance by the family members toward the new culture slows down the acculturation and language acquisition process, and puts pressure on available community social services, among which are the public schools. And the public schools are different from many of the other community services. The schools require the children of the newcomers to be physically present in their classrooms during the prime time of the day, and like it or not, the schools are in the business of inducting these young people into the new culture as they participate in the schools' subject matters. In some cases, this learning is viewed as a threat to the adults: either the learning is going to take the children away from them or they may be losing a potential wage earner.

However, the children of the newcomers are required by law to attend the English-speaking schools, so these children must step out of the family comfort zone. In no time at all, the children find themselves uneasily trying to bestride two cultures—the one at home and the one at school. Much the same thing can be said about poverty; the United States has a number of "indigenous cultures," and poverty is one of them. And at the high school level, a third "culture" is nearly always present—cliques within the peer group, with all their pressures, values, and customs. The years between fourteen and nineteen are most assuredly not the most settled in terms of the individual personality. These are the years full of "try-ons"—

experimenting with ways to fit in with the crowd, stand out from the crowd, and discover who one is all at once—and sensing the relentless future fast approaching. All of these things are occurring in bodies that look adult but these students are still children in many ways.

Sound daunting? Well, yes, in a way it is. But the teen years also are full of flexibility, fluidity, and experimentation—the try-ons signal that. As such, try-ons also signal a willingness to try something new and to explore new ways of doing and feeling. And because this age group is composed of students who must spend time together, they inevitably learn to know one another. As an article in *The Washington Post* pointed out, we are headed into what has been termed "post-ethnic America."[2] Postethnicity is seen as reflecting:

> Not only a growing willingness—and ability—to cross cultures, but also the evolution of a nation in which personal identity is shaped more by cultural preferences than by skin color or ethnic heritage. . . .
>
> Today's young Americans represent the most multiracial group in modern American history. According to Census 2000, 40 percent of people under the age of 25—"echo boomers" and younger—belong to some race or ethnic category other than non-Hispanic white.

In other words, it's what you do and what you're interested in that count. Right now, the great mixing bowl is largely located in the big cities, but the inner rings of suburbs are beginning to feel the impact. We see this trend as wonderfully hopeful; perhaps the old, racial divide finally will erode, and maybe W. E. B. DuBois's statement about race being the central issue of the twentieth century will not carry over into the twenty-first.[3] Perhaps, in the United States, the twenty-first century will see productive growth toward postethnicity and a broadened cultural perspective. After all, we are the most diverse nation in the world.

As a teacher at the high school level facing diverse groups of students, you need to recognize your students' search to become, and you need to advocate for postethnicity and a broad cultural perspective. The students will adapt and adjust to one another. They will learn from each other as well as from you; they have to, to survive. But they want to go beyond that: they want to thrive and prevail. You need to set the tone by welcoming everyone, by treating every student with respect and fairness, with an eye to capitalizing on their strengths, even though you will inevitably like some students more than others.

For your part, right from the first day, make the effort to learn their names. Don't anglicize what may be to you a virtually unpronounceable name. One of the authors found out early on the name Hughes can be a horror to pronounce for incoming Latinos, Middle Eastern, and Asian students—Celtic pronunciation rules aren't usually in their lexicons, but the students learned fast. Have the students in question teach you the correct pronunciation and spelling, too, if necessary. Look at each student as a real person and find something beautiful or striking about each one of them, and find a way to communicate your "findings." Find out something about their backgrounds, have them work in small groups if appropriate, and find ways for them to interact and get to know one another. Tell them something about yourself and your subject matter, including its importance to their education and future lives. Assure them of your firm belief in their capacity to learn and that you will help them to do just that. Then, get down to business in your subject matter, but remember to leaven what you do with humor and compassion. It's an odds-on probability you will be on your way to success in teaching these—and now your—students.

THE GREAT TWO-FACED COIN OF TEACHING—BEING A PARTICIPANT-OBSERVER

"So what is this?" you ask, upon seeing this section heading. And we answer, "No, we are not really taking a little detour into social anthropology. Rather, we are translating a well-known role as developed and practiced by anthropologists in conducting and managing their field research into a classroom setting." Curiously, this role as it relates to teaching and learning in a classroom is often overlooked or only dimly understood, but the best teachers will adopt it, even though they may never fully articulate its functions or label it by name.

"All right," you say. "If that is the case, what are its characteristics? How do I do it?" Its principal characteristic is you must be two-faced all the time, like a coin with two faces, in both your teaching and planning. On one side of the coin, you are the lead participant in the learning process of students with regard to your particular subject matter. You are working to communicate what you know, your subject matter, to the students in ways that will allow them to receive and process the incoming message accurately and with enthusiasm. If you are to be effective as a teacher, your participation in the process is, of course, absolutely essential, but it is not enough. Inexperienced teachers tend to focus almost entirely on the first side of the coin. That is, they are so busy trying to put their subject matter across they may lose sight of the extent to which the students are actually receiving it. They are not really observing the students, the other side of the coin.

This other side of the coin, the astute observer, is the more subtle aspect. And it takes practice. You must constantly be processing the messages the students are sending to you, both verbally and nonverbally. It's the nonverbal ones that are often the most telling. In short, you must accurately observe the incoming behaviors from the class like a hawk and then smoothly adjust your participant role to deal with them.

These adjustments have an almost infinite variety to them. For example, they can take the form of minute nonverbal signals, like a hand gesture from you asking a student to wait a moment or two before raising a question so you can finish the last sentence of your presentation. They can occur unobtrusively through adding illustrations to drive across a concept upon seeing puzzled or glazed expressions appear on the students' faces.

As another example, the adjustment may take the form of a full stop when you realize you really have lost them somewhere along. Don't pussyfoot around; come to the point, and ask them, "Where did we part company?" or "Where did I head down a side road while you stayed on the main highway?" If you can interject some humor into your questioning that in no way puts them down, it is the best way. "Oh, man. I guess I was trying to speed up to beat the bell. Mistake!" Or, "You know, I have the distinct feeling I'm engaging in a one-person discussion. Am I right?" Regardless of how you query them, you must be sincere about it, and they must see your questioning as nonthreatening. If they are convinced you are for real, they will tell you. When they do tell you where the difficulty occurred, you must make some immediately recognizable (to them) adjustments of your presentation or activity to solve the problem. Sometimes, you and they will need to have a discussion of the difficulty, and then you can agree upon some form of review, a further explanation, or additional illustrations (frequent activities in statistics, one of us has found). Engaging in these activities will help to build a partnership between you and your students.

Another way to adjust for the difficulty is to have a special session on the particular topic with the students who are experiencing the greatest difficulty, either during a study hall or at the end of a class period. This approach is particularly helpful with new immigrants and limited-English speakers as well as with poor readers, and it can save them from embarrassment in front of their peers. Just hearing the presentation repeated can help.

Sometimes, the adjustment comes in the elimination of some topic in the course that really turns out to be nonessential. Always, the question we ask ourselves, and so should you, is: "What do these students really need to know to pass my course? To be ready for the next course in the sequence?" You may not succeed fully with every student, but each one will know you gave your best shot—and they just may surprise you. It has certainly happened to us.

ASSESSING STUDENTS' LEARNING

Education goes through a lot of fads. The current one seems to be testing, and more specifically, what has been called high-stakes testing. And it has become fashionable with elected officials because it's much cheaper to test than it is to overhaul teacher education or pay teaching professionals at a level commensurate with their importance. Ultimately, these changes in teacher preparation and pay will have to occur, but don't hold your breath waiting for them to happen tomorrow or next year.

For one thing, you must fully realize that your workload has just increased. It's not good enough to be a fine teacher in communicating your subject matter to students and then assessing your students' knowledge of it yourself. You must also prepare them to pass new state-imposed tests in various subject matters regardless of your assessment of your students' readiness to take such tests. Somehow, you must cover the material specified for the subject matter at the particular level you are teaching. What's underlying this mouthful is that even though you may be teaching ninth-grade history and the axe doesn't fall until the twelfth grade, you must manage to teach every topic because you are laying the foundation for other teachers to build on. Here is where the pedagogical techniques of "pruning the course," "accelerate slowly," and "inductive learning" (including "anchoring") are essential.

Here is what we do to assess students' learning.

We provide the students with a syllabus that clearly presents the objectives of the course, the topics to be covered, the essential chapters of the text, other reading involved, projects to be completed, and the test schedule.

A Return Visit to Objectives

Way back in chapter 1, we talked about the need for stating clear and complete objectives for each of your courses and the ways in which such objectives can help you teach and evaluate if you and your students have achieved them. Let us pay a little return visit to this topic, and now our emphasis is on the usefulness of the academic objectives to your own assessment of student learning internally as well as to the externally imposed achievement tests.

The big point is that a few clearly stated objectives for each course will keep you focused on its essential elements. Here are two examples. One has been taken from an introductory physics course, the other from an introductory course in sociology.

For an introductory physics course, there are three overarching objectives. They are:

- To define and illustrate physical quantities through anchoring them to students' experiences.
- To derive the units of the specified physical quantities based on their mathematical definitions.
- To solve problems in physics based on the mathematical definitions of the physical quantities.

The time spent on each of the three objectives is approximately 20 percent, 10 percent, and 70 percent, respectively. This pattern has been followed for each class session.

Similarly, the Introduction to Sociology course has three student objectives.

- To define, analyze, and illustrate major concepts in sociology.
- To learn and apply the major theoretical approaches and terminology of sociology to the study of social systems, phenomena, and problems.
- To examine one major social problem through the methods of social research.

The time spent on each of these objectives was about 35 percent for each of the first two, and 30 percent for the third one over the course of the semester.

The Great Carrot Incentive

Telling students they will have to study hard in order to do well in your courses is going to be received by them as a "drop-dead idea." They have heard it before—thousands of times. You must do better than this—and you can. Here are some ideas that really work.

- Give announced tests often, and tell the students, "None of the tests is comprehensive, including the final test." Let them know they have less to study for each test, and they don't have to go back to the beginning.
- Exempt those students from taking the final test who have an A average on the previous tests. This is a big incentive to motivate students to study right from the start of the course, and they pay attention in class. Typically, final test day sees only about 25 percent of the students having to be there.
- Let the students know what they can expect on the test. Don't pull any surprises. Provide sample tests whenever possible. If that does not work out, discuss the types of topics or problems the students can expect to see on the test. Let the students know that the test will only cover material presented in class, so they need to take good notes and then study them. This practice typically forces them to take adequate notes and to ask questions if the points are not clear.
- Include one or two questions or problems for extra points, amounting to 10 to 20 percent of the main test. If the students miss something on the main test, they can salvage the day by doing well on the bonus questions. We have found that almost every student will complete both the main test and the bonus questions. They are going to take no chances.
- Score and return tests at the next class meeting if at all possible and go over the test with them. If, in your scoring, you discover a bad item (e.g., an unclear or a double-barreled question—one with multiple answers), tell the students that it was a bad item, and exclude it from scoring. This practice sends the students a message that you care and you are fair. Oddly enough, they start wanting to do well for you, and so they set higher expectations for themselves.
- Let your objectives drive the course and the tests. For example, in the physics course earlier alluded to, the make-up of the tests reflects the time distribution spent on the definitions, the units, and the problems. In sociology, the tests overall reflect the time distribution. But if one

of the three major elements comprising the objectives is going to pre-
dominate on a particular test, the students are alerted to this and the
reasons are given for it well in advance of the test day.

- Give students the grade they have earned in accordance with your cri-
teria. If everybody merits an A, make sure everybody receives one. Do
not be conned into believing you have practiced grade inflation. What
you should do, however, is congratulate yourself on having done dyna-
mite teaching and congratulate the students on achieving a dazzling
performance. Be mindful that a predetermined grade distribution is a
sure sign of weak teaching, and it's a cop-out, too, which is even worse
than weak teaching.

By now, you have seen the positive approaches to be taken in your assessment of students' performances, and you have given valuable practice in
test taking and in succeeding on a test. This experience will serve them well
as they prepare for the achievement tests as they come up to graduation.

USING TECHNOLOGY IN THE CLASSROOM—A
DOUBLE-EDGED SWORD

Technology is here, and you as a teacher should make use of it. However,
the chances are that some of your students may be more proficient in it
than you are. Before we discuss its usage, we want you to answer some
questions. How proficient are you in the use of technology yourself? Does
your subject matter immediately suggest some productive uses of computer
applications for the students or for you? How well equipped is your school?
Do your students have access to a computer at home, at the home of a
friend, or in the after-school program? The answers you give here must be
factored into your preplanning for your courses and into your teaching as
well. If you are answering no to any of these questions, you have a problem.
You need to postpone any real use of the computer until you can supply
"Yes's" to all of them, particularly the question about your own proficiency.

Bear in mind the use of technology in classroom teaching is a double-
edged sword. Let us look at the plus side first. Both the capability and novelty of the new technology equipment definitely should encourage you as a
teacher to want to use the equipment in your classroom. Teenagers love
new stuff, but the novelty and capability are not enough. Another point you
must consider is, "Will the equipment really enhance the students' learning

of the topics in the courses I'm teaching?" If you're answering yes to this query, then the last question becomes, "Am I qualified or comfortable in using a particular computer program in the teaching of my course topics?" If the answer is yes again, then you should go ahead and factor in the use the computer. Case 12.1 provided below illustrates these points. The topic involves creating an automatic outline on the computer.

CASE 12.1

I introduced the task of preparing a research paper, and I wanted the students to prepare their outlines for the paper using a word processor on a computer. For this task, I, as the teacher, made certain that I understood all aspects of the outline in a particular word processing program and then took the students to the state-of-the-art computer lab where *every* student had access to a computer.

Prior to using the computer for producing an outline, I had already made certain the students knew how to create an outline in longhand. I issued step-by-step instructions for creating a three-level outline on the computer and made certain every student was with me. The outlines were practiced through making changes that involved inserting and deleting items in the original outline in accordance with their research problems. Once I approved the outlines, I showed them how to make a template for their future outlines. In addition, I encouraged the students to use the Internet, the university's library, and the electronic databases of the consortium libraries to track down appropriate materials for their papers.

One last caveat: Students should not be trying to learn what is required for a research paper outline *and* how to use the computer's outlining capabilities at the same time. These tasks should be done *ad seriatim* and not in tandem. One step at a time, please!

Another example for the plus side is the use of Excel spreadsheets for the analysis of laboratory data (Case 12.2).

CASE 12.2

I used the Excel program for every laboratory in the introductory college physics courses. A sample of a finished project work is provided in figure 12.1.

Before students went to the computer laboratory to use the Excel program for data analysis, they had taken observations on the length of the pendulum and the time for fifty oscillations at least five times. They entered the data in appropriate cells. After entering the data, the formulas were used to calculate the time for one oscillation, the value of g and its average, and the percent error.

During this period, I discovered that a student who was having a difficult time with the course happened to possess excellent skills in the use of Excel. I placed her in charge of the data analysis part in the computer laboratory. This created tremendous confidence in this particular student's ability. As a result, she started improving in the rest of the course, and eventually aced the course.

Although technology has many advantages in improving students' ability to do well in a course and handle difficult tasks, we must reiterate again that as a teacher, wanting to use a particular program, you must really know the ins and outs of it. Case 12.3 illustrates the minus side of a computer program if you are not comfortable in its use. The classroom is not the place for you, the teacher, to fumble around and learn the program in front of students or peers.

In spite of all the advantages technology offers, there is another minus

	A	B	C	D	E	F
1	Experiment 4: To determine the value of acceleration due to gravity (g)					
2	using a Simple Pendulum					
3						
4	S.N.	Length of the Pendulum (cm)	Time for 50 oscillations (sec)	Time for one oscillation (sec)	g (cm/sec^2)	Average g (cm/sec^2)
5						
6	1	82.20	90.30	1.81	995.74	
7	2	90.70	95.20	1.90	988.51	
8	3	101.50	101.50	2.03	973.16	985.19
9	4	111.50	105.70	2.11	985.77	
10	5	119.30	109.50	2.19	982.79	
11						
12						
13						
14	Percent Error		0.53%			
15						

Figure 12.1. Use of a Spreadsheet in a Physics Laboratory

CASE 12.3

I was a participant in a workshop held at a local university. Although PowerPoint was an appropriate computer program to use to present the information to this audience, the presenter didn't know the difference between two critical features of the program, the "Slide View" and "Slide Show" modes, essential to the presentation. The presenter was calling for technical help for every detail of operation in PowerPoint until I bailed her out. This need by the presenter for help was repeated when the remote-control computer mouse was used. In the meantime, other participants left the room to make a phone call, use the restroom, or just smoke—they became kind of impatient. The impact of the information and the features of the PowerPoint program in action went from dazzle to fizzle.

to it. It becomes apparent when we fail to consider if a particular computer program will enhance student learning or not. You must determine when the use of technology is not going to enhance students' learning even when the program appeals to you and you are an expert in its use. Let us return to PowerPoint to illustrate our point.

We mentioned earlier that PowerPoint, by and large, is a wonderful program when you are making presentations to your peers or your students. PowerPoint presentations are suitable for the conference room, a student competition at a science fair, and reporting a research study to peers. However, its suitability is questionable for classroom teaching because it basically reduces students to passive learners, and it usually doesn't allow sufficient time for adequate note taking. The same point can be made in regard to an earlier technology, transparencies or an overhead projector, when teaching accounting or some other subject matter. Putting it altogether, PowerPoint is not an interactive program, and it may not help when you are teaching a course.

By all means, you should consider using the computer where appropriate in your courses, but be judicious in its use. Remember you are teaching your particular subject matter and not the computer program *per se.*

RESOURCES AVAILABLE TO YOU AND YOUR STUDENTS

As a teacher, you need to become acquainted with the academic and academic-related resources available to assist you and your students in your immediate school, in the school system as a whole, in the neighborhood, and in the city or region in which you are based. Usually, a school or a school district will prepare a packet of materials describing available services. Among these are the free lunch program, school cafeteria, ESL program or courses, health services, kinds of laboratories available, library services and their locations, sports opportunities, guidance counseling services, subject matter consultants and, perhaps, mentors, math and reading tutoring programs, after-school programs, school clubs, and PTA activities.

If your school doesn't provide a listing or such a packet, then you will need to visit the "front office" and find out what is available to you and your students—particularly if you are a newcomer. Don't stop with just finding out what is available; find out whom you should contact either by phone or e-mail. While you're there, inquire about the policy and procedures for field trips, and start planning some to enrich your courses. All too often, newcomers to a school system don't have these opportunities pointed out to them. Moreover, if you are a newcomer who is teaching poor and/or diverse students, you may overlook the opportunities available to you and your students. Ask questions, and then ask some more questions.

All of this is for openers. You also will need to learn what resources are present in the immediate area in which your school is located. Typically, there will be meeting places, like churches (often the site of ESL and tutoring programs) and recreation or senior centers that often run programs of interest. You should know where the nearest police and fire stations are, and they, too, may offer youth programs. The local shopping area is important because there may be opportunities for your students to apply for part-time jobs. Maybe there's even a branch of the public library close by, and that is a job source, too. Drive around the school's neighborhood to see what the living in the neighborhood is like, how the residences look, who's out on the street, the conditions of the residences and business section. A self-guided tour will tell you a lot about the lives your students lead. You don't have to live in the neighborhood or like it, but you need to have some understanding of it if you are to be an effective teacher of your students who do have to live there.

Then look at the city or region. What's available to you and your students? Museums? Theaters? Parks? Historic sites? Libraries? University facilities? Recreational facilities? Sports? Some occasional events of real interest and educational value to your students? Select the ones that are most relevant to your subject matter and the lives of your students, and start planning to use some of them. A lot of these attractions will be free. If your investigation reveals there is a charge for an activity or field trip of real interest and the students cannot pay, then find someone or some organization to contribute. Your principal or the school PTA might be very helpful here in targeting donors or knowing whom to contact.

Case 12.4 is an instance of taking advantage of a special event in Washington, D.C., a veritable gold mine for such events. The subject matter was sociology, and the event was the Million Man March in the late 1990s, organized by the Black Muslims to show the black adult male as a strong and caring human being. The event was free.

CASE 12.4

In my two sections of introductory sociology, some of my black male students were particularly interested in the Million Man March. They wanted permission to attend and offered to prepare a report to present to the class as a special assignment. As they spoke, it suddenly struck me: here was a wonderful opportunity for everybody in the two classes to participate in "living a piece of history." So I said to the students, "Let's build on your idea. How about everybody in the two classes attending the march? We can construct a short interview schedule to find out how the marchers feel about the idea and their own individual participation." The students were delighted with the use of their idea.

That evening, these students presented the expanded idea to both classes. Only a few students, new immigrants from Asia, were a bit reluctant. But when they found out they would be members of interviewing teams, their reservations evaporated. For the next session, both classes were combined so we could design the interview. After that, we practiced how to approach potential respondents, including being sure to show university identification and guaranteeing a respondent's anonymity. The students decided that each team would conduct somewhere between five and nine interviews. In addition, I then contacted the march organizers about sending teams of UDC students to interview the marchers. They were very much interested and thought it was a good idea. We were off and running.

The big day came, and the students and I went to the march. The Mall between the Capitol and the Lincoln Memorial was packed with people who had participated and now were gathering to hear the speeches. One team had a petite Vietnamese student as a member whose presence was (rather negatively) questioned by one of the marchers: "So what are you doing here at our march?" She was scared, but her team members were not. They defended her presence, and the marcher apologized. He then went on to introduce her and her team to his colleagues. All of the other teams were enthusiastically received, and the marchers were much impressed by college students coming to interview them. (I let the students know I would attend the march on my own, so we would all share the experience. I did so, and was welcomed.)

Upon returning to campus, we agreed it had been for all of us a moving experience, and then we related the experience to the concepts of race, class, and power in the United States. We analyzed our data and summarized our findings. Ultimately, we reported the study and its results on the university's FM radio station.

The five constants as described here can be viewed as a rich environment or landscape in which to practice your profession. If you don't know your landscape, both you and your students will be traveling across a terrain full of potholes, swamps, and thickets. Along the way, some of your students will probably get lost or pushed out. Even if you and the students persevere, the whole experience will be one that everyone will want to forget. However, if you spend time and learn the landscape, you will find your path will smooth out and you will see some memorable sights. All of you will share in a picnic at the end. And everybody will remember they had a blast.

NOTES

1. D. S. Khatri and A. O. Hughes, *American Education Apartheid—Again?* (Lanham, Md.: Scarecrow Press, 2002).

2. Joel Kotkin and Thomas Tseng, "Happy to Mix It All Up," Outlook, *Washington Post* (June 8, 2003), B1, B4.

3. W. E. B. DuBois, *The Souls of Black Folk* (Avenel, N.Y.: Gramercy, Library of Freedom Series, 1994).

13

PINNACLES OF TEACHING: TEACHABLE MOMENTS AND LEARNING MOMENTUM

Now we come to the psychological payoff of teaching and learning: *teachable moments* that are sudden high points but are often ephemeral, and something we have labeled an incremental process, *learning momentum* that builds up steadily in a course toward an unexpected high point. Both add up to the pinnacle of teaching, climbing to the top of the mountain. And like the view from the mountaintop, they are exhilarating and wonderful.

First, let us define what we mean by the teachable moment.

To us, a teachable moment is both a challenge and an opportunity that arises as a result of some incident, event, or statement that is of great interest or significance to both you and your students. These moments are not planned; they occur by chance. They carry risk with them because you must respond quickly and appropriately. The students can learn something of inestimable value to them as a result of your teaching if you are able to capitalize on this window of insight. The opportunity to recognize when you can make a difference in the learning of students in your discipline becomes critical. The teachable moment is both a heightened experience for students to learn and a critical insight for you into the whole teaching-learning process. It *is* the *raison d'être* of teaching.

Let's look at the components of the teachable moment. Something happens either in or outside of the classroom that serves as a trigger. How do you recognize its presence? Sometimes the signals are obvious. An event occurs, like a declaration of war, and the students may ask your opinion. Or a classmate is taken ill or suddenly dies, and the students are noticeably upset by the situation. One or another of them may comment or ask a question. They are struggling not only with why but also with the fragility of life

itself. And because they are younger than you are, they are likely to perceive serious illness or death as something remote from them, unless they
live in neighborhoods where violence and death are frequent occurrences.
When it is this latter situation, you must stress the value of life, and the
right to live it.

Sometimes the signals are subtle. A student may couch a racial or ethnic
slur in the form of a stereotype or joke; some of the students may laugh
while others look uncomfortable. One student may knock another student's
materials on the floor as if by accident, and then snicker with a few other
students at the "accident." Another signal is when you or, perhaps, a student says something that really catches everyone's attention, and the body
language and sudden alertness suggest a need to follow up with some comment, explanation, or discussion. Or the signal may be one of puzzlement
or even indifference to a concept or process you consider important. For
you as a teacher, whatever the trigger, having recognized the signal, the
choice of capitalizing on the opportunity or letting it go is up to you. It is
your decision, and it's not always pleasant. But if the signal is a slur, you
should definitely take action. If you do not—and make no mistake about it,
your status and credibility with the students will be diminished—it's un-
likely that you will be able to recoup.

Now, let us define and examine learning momentum. Learning momentum, unlike the teachable moment, is built slowly and steadily, class session
by class session. It is deliberate, it is planned, and the only real risk in it is
if you can close the gap between where the students must begin and where
you want them to be at the end of the course. However, you will know
when you have achieved your vision when a student (or the students as a
whole) experiences an unexpected academic success. We call this the "aha"
phenomenon, because it is such a surprise to them, and it's wonderful when
it happens to one of them or all of them—and to you.

It usually begins with a kind of vision in your mind somewhat similar to
that of an architect's sketch for a building before laying out a blueprint. In
your case, the vision should consist of students really being able to succeed
in the course whether they believe it or not. This vision requires you to
communicate it to the students and to show them how it's going to be done
through the teaching activities of the class and the students' participation
in them. As the class proceeds, your blueprint begins to take on reality not
only in your mind but slowly and unobtrusively in the students' minds as
well, similar to an architect creating a real building. That is, they begin to
think they can handle the demands of the course as you have defined them.

The first reality check of the initial vision comes when the students do, indeed, succeed in a meaningful course event, often a test. In the architect's case, it is parallel to the building beginning to take shape.

When all—or almost all—of the students actually have succeeded in passing the course, your vision has become a reality for you and for them.

How do you manage the opportunity and the challenge confronting you? Both the teachable moment and learning momentum draw heavily upon those social and academic traits and beliefs you as a person carry with you into the classroom, as well as your subject matter and pedagogical techniques. The four most critical ones are sensitivity to and respect for your students, your ability to be an astute participant-observer, the verbal ability to convey a significant message to the students in a convincing way that deepens and broadens their insights, and the demonstration of your own deep commitment to teaching and learning.

Cases 13.1 and 13.2 are teachable moments in the social sciences. Cases 13.3, 13.4, and 13.5 demonstrate the learning momentum phenomenon (the "aha" phenomenon) first for the students and then for the teacher. Yes, these really do occur for teachers, too.

I ASKED. HE TOLD.

Case 13.1 occurred at the first class meeting of a night section of an introductory sociology class. Classes held at this hour tend to attract older students who work full-time during the day although there are younger students attending as well. The class makeup in this case was predominantly African American; a few Asians from Vietnam, Sri Lanka, Cambodia, and Taiwan; several students from Africa; and one student from Sweden.

CASE 13.1

First, I introduced myself, went over the syllabus, and had students sign a sheet and then write their names on individual sheets of paper so I could learn their names as rapidly as possible. Then, I began the third item on the agenda, "Forces that have shaped us." I noted that sociology views individuals as being molded by key institutions, such as family, schools, the workplace, and events, such as the civil rights movement or an economic depression, in the environment. All of these are forces that shape us. In turn, we play a role, usually in some collective form, in effecting changes and adjustments in those institutions and events. After this explanation, I asked the students to note down three forces they personally thought had been of major significance in shaping them as individuals.

After giving a minute or two to jot down their thoughts, I began calling on the students by name, using the informal "name cards" they had hung over their desks. Predictably, many of the students noted their families and the importance of the schools they attended. Some mentioned their churches. However, the Vietnamese students all stated war and its aftermath as the key force for them, and they described the impacts eloquently, even with their somewhat limited English. The class was fascinated.

But the real attention-getter of the evening came from a good-looking young African American in his early twenties who stood up and announced he came from a military family and had been deeply affected by the civil rights movement. Then he commented, "I came out of the closet last week—I finally told my family I'm gay. It wasn't . . . easy. It's a main force in my life."

An absolute silence fell upon the room, followed by some quick intakes of breath. The students immediately swung from looking at him to studying me, waiting for my response. In a quiet but very clear voice, I said, "You have shown a great deal of courage in telling your family and us as well." I paused, looked around at the silent faces, and then said, "I'm sure you must also have felt a great sense of relief at having done so." I encouraged him to talk about his situation if he felt like doing so because the black community has not been particularly receptive to gays. The class listened avidly and respectfully to what he had to say. I thanked him, and then we moved on to hear what the remaining students had to say.

The message I had sent to the students was one of my own tolerance, respect, and appreciation for the valuable contribution and individuality of each member of the class. At the same time, I was letting them know that no other behavior would be acceptable in this class. They understood and respected that. In subsequent class sessions, he was simply a respected and valuable member of the class. Indeed, the incident seemed to link the class together.

EXAMPLE OF "I"

Case 13.2 comes from an introductory social science class in which the disciplines of physical and social anthropology were being presented and discussed. The students were struggling a bit with the concepts of dominant and recessive genes in human evolution and their political impact in culture as well. How to make it real for them? It all seemed terribly abstract.

CASE 13.2

Suddenly, I had an idea. As the only white in the class, I announced, "I can be viewed as a case study in recessive physical traits." The students looked extremely startled—the reaction I was seeking. Now I had their full attention. I then announced, "I have fair skin, blue eyes, blond hair, and I am small." Then I pointed out, "In contrast, most of you have the dominant physical traits: darker skin, brown or black eyes, dark hair, and are much taller, for the most part, than I am."

Then I went on to comment on the social implications. "In the period of the Roman Empire some 2,500 to 1,500 years ago, members of the ruling elite were dark-haired, dark or olive-skinned, with brown eyes, and generally of medium height. But beyond the boundaries of the empire to the north, there were the folks who looked more like me in terms of their coloring, and they were termed barbarians and definitely not of the power elite. In fact, they needed to be contained." After the students thought this over and asked a few questions, one of them asked, "So do the desirable traits really depend a lot on who's in power? Who controls?" To which I could answer, "Yes, for the most part. You see, race is a cultural phenomenon, and so are the positive and negative associations that come to be attached to it."

The discussion continued, and one of the students joked, "That's why you're in power here as the professor, and we're the students. Is that right?" We all laughed, and I said, "Right. But the situation is only temporary here."

A week later, the students aced the quiz dealing with anthropology and culture.

The message being sent here was that differences in physical traits really didn't matter to me. I viewed the desirability of one set of such traits over another as essentially a nonissue, an unfortunate cultural construct when it comes to ability and talent. The only real issue was power—and its use and abuse. The students quickly perceived I was no racist and that I simply didn't care what they looked like.

THE STUDENT "AHA" PHENOMENON IN A PHYSICS COURSE

As mentioned earlier, the learning momentum phenomenon also can take infinite forms when you are teaching. Three such *current* instances (taken from the 2002–2003 academic year classes) are cited here (Cases 13.3, 13.4, and 13.5).

Case 13.3 took place during the fall semester of 2002 when I was teaching the first part of the course in introductory physics. In the beginning of the course, students were scared and made it clear that they perceived the course to be very difficult, and they said so. And they also noted, based on the reports of other students and what they themselves knew about physics, they were not at all sure if they would pass the course the first time or would even stay in the course for the whole semester.

CASE 13.3

On day one of the course, I passed out an agenda, discussed the students' and my expectations, presented the surprise objectives, and said their predecessors had done well in the course. One student said, "You got to be kidding." Another student said, "Oh, yeah, right." Another student interjected, "Wait a minute. I heard the same thing from some other students—he [the teacher] means what he's saying." The students left the class still feeling dubious.

They listened politely, but they didn't believe it, I could tell. Along about day two, an incredulous student commented, "You know, I really understood what was taught today." The other students looked a little startled, but some of them started nodding their heads. But they still weren't sure they really believed they had understood. They just weren't convinced they could do it, but they kept on coming to the class. Slowly, they began to realize that they really were understanding what was being taught, as evidenced by their answers to my questions. By the time the first test was due, I noticed that everybody took notes, had begun to ask questions, and had lost some of their shyness. During the last class before the first test, I used the agendas for the past four weeks to identify the topics they must study and problems they must practice. Thirty percent of the problems were identified as test problems.

The test day came. All of the students were there for the test. Everybody completed the test. I graded the papers and returned the papers at the next class period.

The reaction of the students was beautiful to behold. Some of them were jumping up and down. A number of students said, "I can't believe it!" "I did so well." "Wow! I did it!" "Oh, my god, I passed! I PASSED!!"

Once the joyous pandemonium subsided, I walked around the class and asked each student, "How long did you study?" Their responses varied, but what came across in the answers to this question was a range from about ten to nearly thirty hours. One student said, "I packed off my husband and kids to my mother's house for the weekend."

Then I asked, "What did you think of the test?" They all agreed that it was fair. One student noted, "It was just as advertised." Finally, I asked, "Do you have any suggestions for improving the construction of the test?" In general, they answered, "Don't change a thing."

Everything came together when they saw their test scores; they had become believers. From then on, we were on a roll. And I could begin to pick up speed in the course.

When I walked in the classroom on the last teaching day of the course, I was absolutely startled to see a cake and all sorts of soft drinks on the table. The students had arranged to celebrate their excitement and delight at having succeeded in the course. The whole class was bubbling with energy. They celebrated their success with a cake-cutting and picture-taking ceremony. I cut the cake, the students took group pictures, and everyone enjoyed the cake and the drinks. After the celebration was over, the class continued—there was one final topic to be completed. The thirteen students who were exempted from the final test were free to go at this point. However, they simply went out in the hallway and waited for the class to end. The remaining five stayed to hear what they would face on the final test, but were confident they would do well. When the session was finished, all thirteen of the "hallway students" trooped back in to continue the celebration. There were big smiles everywhere, accompanied by comments about how much they enjoyed the class.

The experience of success with the first test changed it all for these students for the rest of the semester. They were more comfortable and started feeling that after all physics is not so hard and they could manage to get through the course. Their comfort level in the course and their excitement about it climaxed when they decided to celebrate their success and confidence with the teacher by bringing a special cake. The cake is shown in figure 13.1.

The second instance of the "aha" phenomenon (Case 13.4) occurred during the fall semester of 2003 and is next described for an individual student.

EPIPHANY FOR A TEACHER

Figure 13.2 shows the categorizing of the students' responses into most of the pedagogical techniques described in this book. Eighteen respondents gave at least five answers to the question on teaching techniques.

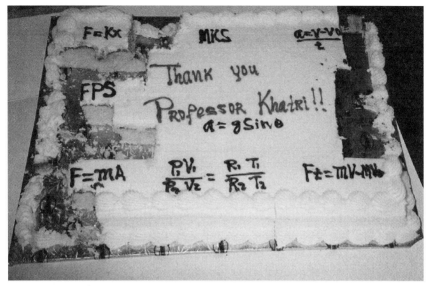

Figure 13.1. Students' End of the Semester Celebration with a Special Cake

Some sample responses from different students are included after the presentation of figure 13.2.

"Repetition is the key." (Stated repeatedly)
"The more you practice the problem, the more you begin to grasp the principle or concept [involved]."
"The real-life examples were very helpful." (Stated repeatedly)
"Open to any and all suggestions and questions from the class."
"Corrected homework returned on the following class day."
"Outlining the chapter with a handout, then executing the daily lesson along the lines of the handout content; this organization helped greatly!!!"
"[He] remained informal, loose, relaxed, and humorous in teaching style and asked students to come to the board more when they seem not to understand the subject content."
"Using pamphlets [agenda] instead of a book to outline the chapters."
"Outlining what is to be expected on the test and ensuring students have the correct information and all the information needed to answer questions properly."

CASE 13.4

This physics class had nineteen students. I gave the first test in late September. One of my students, a very attractive black female about forty-five years old, failed this test. She had no prior background in physics, and she was, at best, shaky in algebraic functions. But she was committed; after discussing the test with her, I asked her to rewrite it several times. In doing so, she figured out where she made "wrong U-turns" in problem solving, definitions, and stating units of physical quantities. I also provided her with a model paper of one of her peers (name removed) as a check. She appeared to gain increased confidence after she wrote this paper several times. On a subsequent test, she earned a C. Once again, I repeated the same process.

I gave the third test during the month of November 2003. There was a surprise waiting for me; she had written a perfect paper and earned an A⁺. After passing all the papers out to the students, I asked them for an evaluation of the class and the teaching methods used in the course. When this student started to describe her experiences in the class, she was so happy she started to cry, and stammered, "This has never happened to me before, and I learned so much in the class, I can't believe myself!"

"Review of basic algebra [on the first and second day of class] was most effective."
"Having homework assignments that weren't lengthy but went straight to the point."
"I don't think I could have survived physics without him. Came to every class."

❊   ❊   ❊   ❊   ❊

Well now, we're almost to the end of our journey. And we are ending our book by showing you the twin pinnacles of teaching. How will you know when you've reached them? You'll know because the students will tell you. Sometimes, it will be directly; other times, it will be through the way your students perform. But it doesn't hurt to ask them directly for their views and comments on what has been productive for them. As we've noted here and there along the way, they are amazingly astute observers. And their nonverbal behaviors are always very revealing, too.

STUDENTS' EVALUATION FOR AN INTRODUCTORY PHYSICS CLASS		
Spring Semester 2003 (N=18)		
Identification of Pedagogical Technqiues		
Pedagogical Techniques	**Frequency**	**Percents**
Teaching Principles		
Anchoring	8	44
Accelerate Slowly	4	22
Practice	14	78
Management Tactics		
Pruning the Course	8	44
Preparing an Agenda	4	22
Sequencing--Divide Problems into Steps	6	33
Review, Re-teach	5	28
Note-Taking	5	28
Equal Student Participation/Calling Students by Name	10	56
You Are Teaching--Not the Book (Teaching Style)	18	100
Complex Teaching Constants		
Assessment	10	56
Other		
Importance of Attendance	4	22

Figure 13.2. Students' Evaluation for an Introductory Physics Course

We want to add that as you become an increasingly better teacher, the more frequent will be the occurrence and realization of teachable moments. We reiterate you can recognize and capitalize on teachable moments, but you cannot predict them. With time and effort, however, all of your courses will probably come to reflect what we have called learning momentum (Case 13.5).

And there will be some other positive effects as well. First, your students will want to do well in the course because they know what your expectations are, and they don't want to let you down. They often will go to great lengths to justify your faith in them and your effort on their behalf. Another effect

CASE 13.5

Another current instance of learning momentum occurred during the spring semester of 2003 when I was teaching the second part of introductory physics. But this time, I was the one who experienced the "aha" phenomenon—thanks to my students. The course was proceeding along smoothly when I had the idea about asking my students about the pedagogical techniques used in this course. I hasten to add, the reader should keep in mind the teaching techniques had never been mentioned in the class.

I prepared my own evaluation instrument. (My coauthor and I were deep in the throes of writing this book.) Some of the questions were routine, such as "What grade do you think you'll receive in this course?" However, the key question was not routine. And the students had to write their own responses—not a favorite tactic to use with diverse and minority students. This question was, "Write the five *most effective* teaching techniques you found most useful in learning the course content."

The students had fifteen minutes to complete the instruments, and they really got into it. They wrote and wrote and wrote. When they had finished, I picked up the papers and asked them about the possible teaching techniques they had identified. They just talked a little about what they had written, and I remember thinking they were quite observant. But the real "aha" did not occur until I sat at my desk and read through their evaluations. Suddenly, it hit me: they hadn't missed a single teaching principle. Of course, they didn't use the formal language, but their observations were right on the money. They had demonstrated they were first-class participant-observers in their own right.

Two days later, I shared their evaluations with my coauthor. She was amazed at the sophistication they displayed in their responses as well as their identification of many of the teaching techniques. She also commented that almost nobody mentioned the lecture technique. When two of them did so, it was in connection with student participation.

After discussing the incident, we decided to include their insights in this book.

is that your reputation as a fine teacher will precede you. Students will strive to enroll in your classes because other students whom you have taught have spread the word.

Finally, when the students have reached their pinnacles of learning, you will have reached yours in teaching. And that's success!

FINALE

Attention, class.
The new color-blind teacher is being created right now.
Are you a candidate?
The prize is rewarding.
The goal is attainable.
We've shared what we know.
It's up to you.
Class dismissed!

INDEX

ABOUT THE AUTHORS

Daryao S. Khatri taught at Jamia Millia Islamia, Department of Physics, India, from 1968 to 1970, and received the highest evaluations from students who came from all walks of life. Since 1973, he has taught diverse populations in all classes at the University of the District of Columbia in the departments of physics and computer science with student retention rates in the vicinity of 95 percent and received the highest evaluations from students and faculty. He is the coauthor of a recently published book, *American Education Apartheid—Again.*

During his tenure as a professor and a project director at the University of the District of Columbia, he and Dr. Anne Hughes secured in excess of $6 million in the form of about fifteen educational and research grants from the U.S. Department of Energy, the National Science Foundation, the Department of Defense, National Institutes of Health, the U.S. Department of Agriculture, and the Digital Equipment Corporation. The major focus of these grants was to research alternative strategies to traditional teaching that could improve the learning of minority students and hence their retention rates at the college level. Similar research was carried out with District of Columbia public school juniors and seniors from two inner-city poor black schools. These grants were built on classroom teaching experiences and research findings from the grants.

During the 1980–1988 time frame, he trained college faculty from various disciplines in the use of mainframe computers and the related application software that was useful to them. The training was carried out for a period of approximately twelve weeks, six hours a week; in turn, prepared faculty became trainers themselves. Since 1989, he has prepared hundreds of training manuals for personal computer training in the areas of databases, spreadsheets, word processing, Internet, professional presentations, and programming languages; many of them were edited by Dr. Hughes. During the mid 1990s, he trained high school students with the intent of studying the impact of high technology on the academic performance of minority students from the poorest neighborhoods. Since 1989, he has trained students and employees in productivity software on personal computers.

Since 1979, the grants were mostly jointly authored, managed, and completed with Dr. Hughes. Dr. Khatri holds a PhD in physics with emphases on mathematics and computer science from the Catholic University of America, and he earned a BSc with honors and an MSc in physics from the University of Delhi, India, in 1966 and 1968 respectively.

Anne O. Hughes, as an assistant professor at the University of Texas (Austin), set up and directed the university's reading clinic, testified before the state legislature on reading disabilities, and worked on research projects in readiness testing, design and teaching of reading materials, and English as a Second Language to first-grade Mexican American children in the ghetto schools of San Antonio. Later, as an associate professor at the University of Arizona (Tucson), she did research on training teachers to work with Mexican American and Indian children at the primary grade levels, and served as a consultant to several tribes with regard to Head Start.

She served briefly in the federal service in education, working with the black community in the Anacostia section of Washington, D.C., and helped design a community school project involving elementary, middle, and senior high schools. She also testified before the U.S. Congress in support of the Anacostia Project. Dr. Hughes was the chief editor of the federally sponsored *Urban Education Task Force Report*, which was entered into the Congressional Record and later published by Praeger.

From there, she served as a professor to the Federal City College, now the University of the District of Columbia, as director of Freshman Studies and assistant provost. During this time, she coauthored a book with John F. Hughes, *Equal Education: A New National Strategy*, published by the University of Indiana Press. At UDC, she served in many capacities, but has always focused on a predominant core: social research, social statistics, tests and measurement, learning theories, and reading in the content field. Along the way, her long association with Dr. Khatri began in 1979, when they established professional seminars for faculty and collaborated on research and demonstration projects. To this core were added high-level critical analysis courses (reading and writing) in the social sciences and sociology courses. All through this period, they collaborated on federally funded research and demonstration projects for improving professorial teaching and minority students' performance at both the high school and undergraduate levels and the development and testing of the pedagogical techniques presented and demonstrated in this book.

Dr. Hughes received her BA in history-English from Swarthmore College; her MA in educational psychology and reading, University of South Carolina (magna cum laude); and her PhD in educational psychology and reading, University of Chicago (cum laude). She is a coauthor of the ScarecrowEducation book *American Education Apartheid—Again?*